Contents

The European Community

The Challenge of Enlargement

ANNA MICHALSKI
and
HELEN WALLACE

Royal Institute of International Affairs

Published by the Royal Institute of International Affairs
Chatham House, 10 St James's Square, London SW1Y 4LE

© Royal Institute of International Affairs, 1992
First published June 1992
Second edition (revised and enlarged) November 1992

British Library Cataloguing in Publication Data

A CIP catalogue record for this book is available from
the British Library

ISBN 0 905031 56 3)001)64769

Text designed and set by Hannah Doe
Cover design by Youngs Design in Production
Printed and bound in Great Britain by Antony Rowe Ltd

Preface to the first edition

This paper emanates from the European Programme of the Royal Institute of International Affairs under the direction of Dr Helen Wallace. It is the first paper to be published as part of a new RIIA project on 'The European Community: The Challenge of Enlargement'.

The Institute and the authors acknowledge the support for this project from the Swedish Ministry of Foreign Affairs, the Norwegian Ministry of Foreign Affairs, the Confederation of Norwegian Business and Industry, and the Norwegian Shipowners' Association, as well as from the sponsors of the European Programme, in particular Cable and Wireless plc, the Commission of the European Community, the Eurotunnel Group, the Gatsby Charitable Foundation, IBM Europe and ICI.

Warm thanks are due to the many people who have given their time to the authors and commented on the draft text. They have provided an invaluable contribution to this work, but the responsibility for the final text rests with the authors.

London, 3 June 1992   Anna Michalski
                                                            Helen Wallace

Preface to the second edition

As a result of a very positive response to the first edition of this book, which not only exceeded our hopes but put us in the gratifying position of being virtually sold out of copies, we decided that rather than simply reprint, we would attempt to revise, expand and update so as to take into account the main developments since first writing.

The new text thus includes some analysis of the Danish and French referenda – of 2 June and 20 September, respectively – as well as adjustments throughout, where situations and our own thinking have become clearer.

It is surprising how much has happened in the space of a few months. Since we have been writing while events have taken place, we cannot pretend to have taken all these developments into account, but we hope that our new text will present a reasonably coherent picture.

In order to bring out the new edition as fast as possible, we have turned for advice to many quarters. We are especially grateful to officials from Austria, Finland, Norway, Sweden and Switzerland as well as from the EC Commission.

London, 26 October 1992   Anna Michalski
                                                           Helen Wallace

1

An overview

The European Community (EC) stands on the verge of what could prove to be either an exciting and creative adventure or a sapping of time, energy and effectiveness. The EC is going to be enlarged; it is an illusion to believe any longer that there is anything optional about responding affirmatively to at least some of the pressing candidatures, both declared and potential. The choices are about which other European countries to accept, when and on what terms – for *both* them *and* the existing members. This paper surveys some of the issues that are relevant to this debate. In its updated form, it also sets these issues in the troubled context of the Maastricht ratification debate and the fall-out from the currency crisis of September 1992.

The real challenge, then, is about how to ensure both that European Union (still not fully defined) is kept on the road and that enlargement is a success, in the sense of providing added value, politically and economically, to both old and new members. The notion of a choice between widening and deepening, if it ever really existed, is no longer credible. The risk that widening could in practice lead to dilution and dissipation of effectiveness remains real. But to deepen and to exclude reasonable candidates would be an equally dangerous rebuff to other Europeans for whom EC actions, rules and legislation are already the key factors around which they have to orient their policies and politics.

Beyond hovers another crucial test for the EC: namely, how to respond to the needs of yet other dependent European states and neighbours which cannot in the medium term, or perhaps the longer term, realistically aspire to full EC membership conventionally defined. Their dependence on the EC is not likely to diminish; indeed it will grow as the EC enlarges. No universally acceptable definition of who are Europeans and who are not is likely to rescue the EC from the dilemma of where to draw its eastern and southeastern boundaries. In resolving this dilemma by making specific judgments on specific cases at specific times the EC must take great care not to create an underclass of European countries and an unstable periphery of aggrieved dependants. It must take care not to inflame conflicts within those countries where arguments about EC membership are already sensitive factors in the domestic political debate.

But it is equally important that enlargement should not be seen as a catch-all solution to the need to find new relationships with states that are refugees from communist systems, whether in eastern Europe, as we used to define it, or in the republics that used to comprise the Soviet Union. The European Community and Europe need not be coterminous for both to have meaning. Integration and cooperation cannot be elided as concepts without a price being paid, since to weaken the dynamics of political and economic integration within the EC would be to make it less effective at a time when it will have to carry yet greater responsibilities for the economic vigour and political stability of Europe as a whole. The daunting problems of Russia and the fragile polities of its former vassals in Eurasia will not be made more tractable by bringing them within the EC and thus almost certainly prejudicing the achievements of what has until now been west European integration. But for the EC leadership to state honestly and openly that some countries are not (yet – or in the foreseeable future) eligible for EC membership does not absolve them from responsibility for policies of active partnership or from the need to think much harder about how to assist their reform processes.

But whether by enlarging its membership or by developing policies of supportive cooperation, the EC will have to face up to some tough questions about its own priorities and the balance of its policies, as well as about adapting its institutions. The challenge of enlargement should not be met simply by subordinating the claims of candidates to the vested interests of the current insiders. Nor should it be reduced to a patronizing judgment about one or two other countries that might at last be up to the standards of the EC. This time the questions raised by enlargement are core questions of European construction. They demand that the EC have the European policy that has long eluded it. The EC will be judged to have failed by both candidates and the world outside if it does not address these issues.

This time enlargement perhaps also implies that the old model of economic and political integration, set in place for part only of an amputated continent, be reappraised. Such a reappraisal need not be subversive. After all, it is precisely because of the success of west European integration that so many other Europeans claim they want to join in the process. But a framework put in place perforce for only a few countries, and then stretched to double its coverage, will not necessarily prove either elastic enough or robust enough to bear the strain of twenty or thirty members without serious reinforcement *and* some redesign.

Subsequent sections of this paper set out: the implications of recent changes in the EC, as it emerges from the Intergovernmental Conferences (IGCs) that led to the signature of the Treaty of Maastricht on European Union (EU), and the bruising process of ratification; the array of opinions within the EC on the issue of enlargement; brief profiles of the policies and predicaments of candidates, both declared and potential; and some relevant lessons from both previous enlargements and recent EC negotiations with possible new members. The paper does not deal with the very important issues raised for EC policy by the need to contribute to the stabilization of Russia and its non-European associates.

1.1 The need for clear thinking
From the welter of information and inquiry, only briefly summarized in this paper, it is evident that the challenge of enlargement is already prompting some deep searching into the political souls

of both member and not – yet – member countries of the EC. The consequential tensions and conflicts of interest and judgment will make the enlargement debate and the management of policy and negotiations very tricky. Already three mistakes of conceptual category hover in the debate:

1 Some policy-makers and politicians in the EC and in the European Free Trade Association (EFTA), even in Cyprus and Malta too, wish to argue that the next round of enlargement can be just like previous rounds, as regards the eligibility of candidates, the type of negotiation involved and the feasibility of leaving intact the essence of the EC and the interests embedded in it – this is almost certainly an illusion, given the number, character and diversity of potential new members and the prospect of waves of enlargement;

2 Others are tempted to argue that the EC is more or less infinitely extendable to the east and perhaps the southeast – but this is to confuse cooperation and integration and to forget the lessons of the early years of the Council of Europe, which proved to be under-equipped to build a framework of intense integration and burden-sharing;

3 Some in the would-be member states among the new democracies believe that early EC membership, conventionally defined, would respond directly to their needs and could be quickly achieved – but this underestimates the scale of the adjustments required and the constraints that would follow, leaning too much on the Portuguese and Spanish precedents and paying too little attention to the sadder Greek story.

One can already begin to see the contours of the enlargement debate and some of its emerging features. The Maastricht European Council of December 1991 reached three decisions directly relevant to enlargement. First, it produced an agreement to proceed to enlargement negotiations once the new basis for EC financing was endorsed. Second, it asked the Commission to produce a report on the implications of enlargement for the Lisbon European Council of June 1992. Third, it altered the treaty clause on enlargement from the words used in Article 237 of the Treaty of Rome by stating in Article O that 'any European state may apply ... for membership of the Union' (i.e. all three pillars), and restated the need for the 'assent' of the European Parliament. Article F reaffirms that the Union consists of democracies and adds that the Union 'shall respect fundamental human rights'. The presidency conclusions and the separate declaration on enlargement stressed these points, not only to note that any European democracy could apply, but also to insist on the need for a demonstrable respect for fundamental human rights. In addition, the steps agreed to achieve both Economic and Monetary Union (EMU) and European Political Union (EPU) have, of course, raised the integration threshold which new members would have to be willing to cross. However, whatever the doubts that have been expressed in some existing member states about the content of the Treaty on EU, its terms have not deflected any candidate country from pursuing its application.

Before the Commission Report on enlargement could be penned, the context of the debate had dramatically altered. The 'no' vote in the Danish referendum of 2 June 1992 threw into question whether the Treaty on EU could or would be ratified and at the very least delayed the process. One troublesome element in the Danish debate had been the concern lest Maastricht be the thin end of a fat wedge which would erode still further the freedom of manoeuvre of EC member states. Enlargement would, some had argued, require radical institutional reform before the ink on the Maastricht text was dry, and in particular, it was alleged, would necessarily curtail the influence and representation of smaller countries. Thus the political sustainability of the Maastricht package and the relative weighting of member states immediately became contentious political issues.

Acutely conscious of the sensitivity of their task, the drafters of the Commission Report on enlargement, and the Commission itself, opted for prudent and nuanced interrogatives, rather than dogmatic assertion. The report, tabled at the Lisbon European Council in June 1992, endorsed the aim of enlargement with a first 'wave' of Eftans – and indicated that negotiations could be pursued on a relatively straightforward and speedy basis. The conditions to be satisfied were respect for the *acquis communautaire* and the assurance that neutral policies would not nobble the emerging common foreign and security policy (CFSP). The report noted that institutional adaptations would be required, but need not necessarily be radical – yet. The Commission preferred not to rush with a southern enlargement, though it stressed the need for an improved relationship with Turkey, or with an eastern enlargement, but it did emphasize the importance of wide-ranging 'partnership' with central and east Europeans.

The European Council meeting in Lisbon found EC leaders anxious and preoccupied, especially with a Maastricht referendum looming in France as well. They endorsed the Commission Report, stressed that enlargement was an active objective, but reiterated that, first, the Maastricht text needed to be ratified and the so-called Delors-2 package settled. They nevertheless all still expressed the hope that this would permit enlargement negotiations to open early in 1993, while the incoming British presidency reaffirmed its intention to prepare those negotiations during the autumn.

However, in the following months this carefully crafted optimism began to crack, as opinion polls in France demonstrated the volatility of support for further political integration, as Danish doubts persisted, as German public opinion wavered and German worries about EMU became more audible, and as the commitment of the British to Maastricht looked increasingly contested. The crisis occurring within the European exchange-rate mechanism (ERM) in September 1992, barely offset by the narrow 'yes' in the French referendum of 20 September, left EC politicians in some disarray, and contending plans to rescue the situation were exchanged for the extraordinary European Council in Birmingham of October 1992 and the Edinburgh European Council of December. A deeply troubled British presidency, to be followed by a beleaguered Danish presidency, transformed what should have been a phase of constructively pro-enlargement Council leadership into a tense period, which was testing some of the fundamentals of the EC political model.

The budget negotiations over the Delors-2 package and the cohesion fund always risked being both contentious and protracted. There is competition for funding between internal claimants and external dependants. It may be the case that budgetary and enlargement issues will become intertwined, since EC finances now run on a five-year planning cycle. Some assumptions will have to be made sooner rather than later about the likely providers of revenue, i.e. including the Eftan applicants, and the probable clients of EC spending programmes, among which candidates beyond EFTA would necessarily in due course be included. This issue has become all the more delicate since the impact of unification on the (west) German economy has become clearer and more painful, while the reticences of the UK about its position in relation to the EC budget are well known.

International recession and fiscal deficits in EC member states do not provide a favourable climate for budgetary growth. Some who are already payers will have to pay more; some current net recipients will have to become net contributors; and some claimants will have to temper their demands for additional funding. A solution to the budgetary conundrum and agreement on some version of the Delors-2 package will need to be found for the enlargement dossier to move forward at all, and perhaps even already implicitly, if not explicitly, the two dossiers may be linked in substance and not only timing. But neither enlargement nor interim partnership with would-be members can be financially painless in the short to medium term.

What might none the less have been a technical debate about the budget became overshadowed by the more serious question of the sustainability of the EMU project. The negotiators of the Maastricht text always knew that they were playing with fire, and that their plans required demanding commitments from member states and real changes in the European economy. The currency crisis of September 1992 left them with no remaining doubts as to the size and complexity of the enterprise. Loss of political cohesion makes measures of technical economic cohesion and convergence harder to deliver. Worries about protracted recession cause political leaders to turn to domestic preoccupations and introversion – a more difficult climate for intra-EC solidarity, let alone generosity to those outside the club.

1.2 The candidates

'Any European democracy' ... the words invite any country that aspires to both attributes to envisage itself becoming a member of the EC. Reality is much more demanding. It is the existing members who have to determine the conditions of accession, and for the moment the hard additional conditions are acceptance of the *acquis communautaire* and the much less definable *acquis politique* (on which see section 2.1), while the agreement at Maastricht sought to alter the ultimate goals, or *finalités politiques*, of the European Union, to which new adherents would have to subscribe. The tricky area for some candidates, most obviously the neutrals, lies in the development of a common foreign and security policy and its possible extension into a common defence policy.

But it is not enough to agree in principle to these several requirements. Candidates, to be credible, have to demonstrate that they could deliver what they promise in order to achieve the benefits that they seek. For this they need appropriately functioning market economies, legal systems and public administrations, as well as the processes of democracy and a good track record on human rights. Nor will good intention suffice to carry conviction with the doubters within the EC, not least given the history of disgruntled members, notably the UK, or deviant ones, notably Greece. The willingness to show tolerance for diversity may be necessary in a larger Community, but not necessarily to take on board more difficult members. Nor will the EC readily contemplate accepting as a member a country which directly or indirectly generates severe tensions with existing members, hence the difficulty of dealing with the Turkish and (Greek) Cypriot applications. Moreover, the EC would be unlikely to welcome a country that might drag it into confrontation with an awkward neighbour on its borders – thus, for example, Croatia vis-à-vis Serbia, Romania vis-à-vis Moldavia or Ukraine vis-à-vis Russia.

8

Views differ on what constitutes economic eligibility. Here a distinction must be drawn between relative wealth and economic structures. The EC covers a range of poorer to richer states, but might not be keen on having too many poorer or very poor members. No one could pretend that the economies of the three Mediterranean countries which joined the EC in the 1980s were already performing at levels comparable with those of the EC9. Yet both Spain and Portugal have adjusted remarkably fast and have often used the disciplines of EC rules and policies to prosecute their economic adjustments. Greece has had a very different experience. Whatever the force of these precedents, in the current debate some argue that candidates would have first to pass some kind of critical threshold, nowhere very precisely set out, although this argument permeates the Commission's Opinion on the Turkish accession of 1989, as it did the Opinion on Greece in 1976. Others argue that with judicious use of transitional arrangements, as well as some flexible definitions, economic acceptability could be achieved quite quickly by at least some of the new democracies.

These various considerations, however wide the range of debate, begin to sort out the more credible short-to-medium-term candidates from the medium-to-long-term potential candidates. All of the members of EFTA emerge as serious runners for negotiations over accession as of now, with of course some tricky substantive issues to be addressed, a difficult debate on the security/ neutrality issue ahead and, in the cases of Iceland and Norway, a potentially very rough negotiation on fisheries. So far four Eftans have applied – Austria, Sweden, Finland and Switzerland – all of which are comparably acceptable in principle, though presenting different substantive issues for negotiation. Norway would have to be regarded as an acceptable candidate for negotiation, and indeed could with some justification present itself as 'reactivating' its old treaty of accession for updating. Iceland and Liechtenstein would be difficult to exclude from a negotiation, and the Icelanders at least could judge that they had little to lose from testing the ground for accession.

All of the EFTA Seven could also, again in principle, move

through the negotiating agenda for enlargement rather quickly, having already accepted so much of the *acquis* in the texts of the European Economic Area (EEA). Two questions only remain open here in advance of negotiation: first, how many of the Eftans will actually apply; and, second, whether the EC will seek to influence their decisions by, as it were, setting a 'best before' date for EFTA applications. The Swiss decision may already have settled these questions for the EC! But what is also crucial for EC leaders and negotiators to remember is that EFTA countries do not have pliant and gullible publics or quiescent sectoral interest groups. Especially in Norway, where memories of their earlier accession debate remain vivid, the detailed terms of accession will matter too. Of course opinion in applicant countries has to make a balanced judgment on the pros and cons of EC accession or the terms which are negotiated. But on the EC side it is vital to bear in mind that if too high a price is exacted from applicants with overly onerous terms, then it will be much harder to sell those terms within the applicant states.

Three southern European countries have tabled their applications – Turkey, Malta and Cyprus. To cut through a much longer discussion, on the criteria *set out above* only the Maltese application is relatively free from complications about its eligibility for consideration. The Cypriot case is being side-lined for the moment because of the political complications with Turkey and Greece, but would otherwise be hard to ignore, given its rather successful economy and internal political system. Opinion has recently begun to harden within the EC against accepting Turkey as a member state in the near future, with the question of the status of the Kurds within its borders a newly stated barrier. However, its delicate geopolitical position vis-à-vis its Balkan, Arab and Asiatic neighbours, combined with its role as a military ally in the North Atlantic Treaty Organization (NATO) and perhaps soon associated with Western European Union (WEU), show how ill-equipped current forms of association are to provide a politically adequate alternative.

All the other European countries are also some way from meeting the conventional criteria of full eligibility. In principle,

Poland, the Czech and Slovak Federal Republic and Hungary look furthest along the road in terms of their domestic transformation processes and their signed Europe agreements with the EC. The agreement with the Czech and Slovak Federal Republic may have to be adapted in the light of the tensions and possible separation of the Czechs and Slovaks. In practice, Poland's current difficulties suggest that it may be less well advanced along this path in some ways, while Bulgaria could emerge as a more credible candidate quite quickly. The other new democracies have even further to go for one reason or another. The Baltic states look in some ways the next obvious group, though unscrambling their economic production from the Russian will take some time. No doubt there will be political pressures to look at Slovenia and Croatia sooner rather than later.

But the discussion about the central and east Europeans has a different quality to it from the often mundanely phrased commentary on the Eftans or the instinctive aversion to a further southern enlargement or the existing southern members' interest in bringing in other southern countries. Whatever the technical difficulties and practical feasibility of extending EC integration eastwards, it is evident that there is a compelling interest from the side of the new democracies, as well as a welcoming political rhetoric from many within the EC, most vocally from British, Danish and German ministers. The disjunction between the political and the technical levels of discourse confuses perhaps four different points. First is the genuine concern of many people in the EC to show a readiness in principle to include the new democracies in the family, not least because the target of membership could provide a ratchet for the processes of transformation. Secondly, timetables for this becoming feasible have been very blurred because, although harsh realism may suggest that full membership could actually take a long while to achieve, to pin this down too explicitly could conversely diminish its value as either a target or a reassurance. Thirdly, there is the persistent concern elsewhere in the EC that the current British government's keen support for enlargement in general says more for its own reluctance to 'deepen' integration than for its interest in the fortunes of the new democracies. Fourthly, the pull of central and east European countries on the economic hub of the German economy and on the attention of German politicians and public alike is beyond question, leaving the rest of the EC with the question of how far it wants to ensure that the EC's *Ostpolitik* defines Germany's *Ostpolitik*.

These issues crowd into the enlargement debate. Even though the probability is that an eastern enlargement is still some way off, the assumption that it is none the less in the offing bears down on current policy assessments in at least four ways. First, if the central and east Europeans have to be explicitly envisaged as members, then the EC needs to start to think now about how an EC of some 25 or more members might actually operate as regards both policies and process. Secondly, if the Europe Agreements are to be seen as a real stepping-stone, their implementation has to be done in this spirit, and this almost certainly implies a different approach from that pursued in previous association agreements, bearing in mind that long-term promises should not be given casually, as they were in the Greek and Turkish cases. Thirdly, the policy implications of an eastern enlargement suggest a need for changes to existing EC policies way beyond anything prompted by an Eftan enlargement, notably as regards agriculture and financial transfers. And, lastly, the case is already being made for accession by stages for the new democracies (cf. the 'affiliate' membership proposal of Frans Andriessen, echoed in some of the debate in Germany), a fundamentally different approach from the precedents of full membership with varied transitional arrangements in a few difficult areas.

1.3 Timetables

Enlargement may be inevitable, but from the overall EC point of view it is not urgent. Previous enlargements have emerged from protracted negotiations; after all, it took the British over twelve years and the Spanish about eight, although much of the delay in both cases was prompted by French reservations. The recent agreement with EFTA members on the European Economic Area took three and a half difficult years, and in any case might be argued by some in the EC to provide a bridging arrangement that reduces the need for a hasty accession negotiation. All three southern European applicants have association agreements, with provisions not yet fully implemented. The central and east European countries either have, or will soon have, an agreement of one kind or another with the EC. The EC has an established hierarchy of forms of partnership through which it expects associates to move gradually. The EC has also plenty of other internal business to transact and is not in danger of being idle.

However, this time the context is radically different from previous occasions. The number and range of candidates, both declared and in the offing, is more compelling of attention. For the EC to delay may be a sign of weakness and not of strength; indeed some people in both the Commission and the member states believe that the EC has already delayed facing up to the question for too long. The British, German and Danish governments have all expressed a strong preference for early enlargement, as have some Commissioners. The declared EFTA candidates are impatient to start negotiations, especially the Austrians, who have been waiting for a long time, and the Swedes, who have stated explicitly their desire to complete negotiations by December 1993 in order to meet the requirements of their constitution for ratification.

The EC has no interest in being bogged down in iterative negotiations with one candidate or another over the next decade, or in constant disjointed adaptation of its institutions and policies. It also has the opportunity in principle to set out its preferred timetable and to take a view on when and how to phase in its preferred consequential adaptations. Certainly in the first and second enlargements the important questions of transitional periods and subject-specific protocols were looked at together, even though many details had to be looked at country by country.

Five kinds of factor are likely to determine the timetable that emerges. The first is to do with substance. Formal Opinions could be drafted and negotiations completed with most Eftans quite rapidly, since socially, economically and politically they are already very similar to the EC, and some 60% of the *acquis* has already been covered by the EEA, though the EEA example also shows how long even apparently straightforward issues can take to be resolved. The Swedish Opinion was produced speedily in July 1992, with the Finnish to follow in late October and the Swiss towards the end of 1992 or early 1993. Technically negotiations could also be quite quick with Malta and Cyprus. Most other candidates would take much longer and require complex judgments about transitional periods, derogations, special protocols and so on.

The second factor has to do with endorsement and ratification procedures. We know from the EEA experience that both the European Parliament and the European Court of Justice need to be taken into account, the former because of its right to endorse enlargement, which it might want to use as leverage for other purposes, and the latter in case anything unusual emerged in the texts negotiated, e.g. as regards variable geometry or, say, a contested definition of what constituted the relevant *acquis*. In addition, time needs to be allowed for the ratification processes in both existing EC and acceding countries, some of which could be protracted – the Swiss and Swedish cases are relevant here.

Thirdly, a choice has to be made on whether to deal with candidates severally or in batches. If the EC does not want to provoke more applications, it could simply operate responsively; alternatively, it could declare dates by which, say, Eftans now, and a first group of new democracies in perhaps five years or so, would have to express their desire to negotiate.

Fourthly, a judgment will have to be reached on the point at which the adaptation of the EC itself needs to be more than marginal. Already some voices can be heard, especially from London, suggesting that the next group of candidates – two or three or four – could be accommodated within the existing structures and then take part in the next IGC. Those who take a contrary view and exhort more radical changes might want the IGC to precede enlargement. The whole process could then take somewhat longer. An alternative would be to open the preparatory phase for the IGC ahead of 1996 and find a formula for involving countries already *en route* for membership, as in effect happened for the Single European Act (SEA) in 1985.

Finally, a new factor has impinged since Maastricht. The Treaty of European Union is to create new pillars alongside the EC, with treaty-based characteristics and procedures. The question then is with whom or what is the candidate negotiating. Previously there have been Council mandates for the member states to negotiate with candidates, with Commission task forces doing most of the staff work and some of the detailed negotiation for the member states, and periodic high-level political arbitrage by ministers (much of it among themselves) in the Council. Next time, subject to the ratification of the new treaty, candidates will need to be drawn into negotiations about each of the pillars. But in a single negotiating process? With the dossiers prepared both by the Commission and by the Council presidency, with the help of the Council Secretariat? Since there are different views on how self-standing the pillars can or should be, we can expect something of a tussle for primacy on the EC side.

These factors and complications notwithstanding, a first enlargement round could be negotiated in 1993–4, with accession in 1995–6, i.e. around the time when the next IGC is due to be convened. With that to be played out, the real debate on the third stage of EMU to follow and the uncertainties of the reform processes in the new democracies, the balance of probability is that the first round of eastern enlargement would not be negotiated until the end of the decade. Unless... unless, that is, some redefinition of eligibility as regards candidates and of flexibility as regards the EC *acquis* and the seamless web of membership obligations were to be adopted. The Memorandum from the three Visegrad countries – Hungary, the Czech and Slovak Federal Republic, and Poland – tabled before the EC in September 1992, was an attempt to pressure the EC to address those issues sooner rather than later.

1.4 The definition of Community ambitions

The EC is already by far the most important transnational organization in Europe. It is hardly surprising that so many other European countries aspire to be insiders. By and large the remaining European organizations are technical agencies with subject-specific roles to play in the new context. All of a sudden there are fewer that have broad political and economic functions or a security role, and fewer options left for varied patterns of membership. At one end of the spectrum full WEU membership has been defined explicitly as the prerogative of those EC members seriously committed to pursuing a common defence policy. At the other end of the spectrum the Conference on Security and Cooperation in Europe (CSCE), which used to be composed of the European states and the two superpowers, now consists of an array of European and Asiatic countries and embraces the whole of the Commonwealth of Independent States (CIS), with the US still a participant. It is an organization concerned with security issues, broadly defined, in Europe, but it is not a European organization in its composition.

Meanwhile the regional groups with tough rules and clear functions are fast disappearing in central and eastern Europe, following the collapse of communism and as defections multiply. New regional groupings are emerging, but with as yet fluid memberships and loosely defined functions. The only other organization that has a clearly European character and a wide remit is the Council of Europe, its valuable strength focused on human rights issues and its weakness evident in its exhortatory methods and classically intergovernmental features. Both such groupings have useful tasks to fulfil alongside the EC, but much more needs to be done to clarify and perhaps build up the roles of both as part of the reconfiguring of European institutions. Until and unless this happens, the EC will have to bear most of the strain of 'managing' Europe and will remain the focus of the ambitions of countries as yet outside the circle of membership.

But the EC and Europe are not coterminous. It is not only by joining the EC that a country achieves a clear European and democratic identity. Nor are the ambitions of the EC as such about Europe, but rather about turning the EC, at the stroke of 12, into a European Union, and at the same time developing a more effective foreign or external policy towards the rest of the world, other Europeans included. There is thus for the current insiders a tension between their EC and Europe, with some seeing this tension as an enduring antithesis and others bent on removing it.

It is important therefore to identify the different strands of ambition that colour the debate within the EC, in order to see where the scope lies for accommodating enlargement and what needs to be redefined to make enlargement both feasible and successful. The main strands are as follows:

1 Central still to the purposes of the EC is the aim of maintaining a framework better able to deal with some policy issues than can its component parts acting alone, in other words an aim based on self-interest through a framework in which many particular interests are deeply embedded;

2 Increasingly an essential shared purpose is to enhance those interests vis-à-vis others by reinforcing the EC influence exercised internationally, hence the new emphasis on CFSP, especially in the light of the collapse of the USSR and the uncertainties about US leadership;

3 Then there is the goal of completing economic integration, through EMU, and moving forward with political integration, by developing EPU, both of which will be hard to achieve; and

4 Finally there is the absolute requirement of maintaining a Community that is capable of generating effective governance so as to pursue its chosen policies and to build the political agreements needed to sustain them.

To maintain these aims *and* to enlarge is asking a lot of the EC and to risk overloaded circuits. To bring into the EC new members that may be more interested in the achievements of integration than in the pain of generating integration is a risk. To add what might be free-riders could strain too far the fabric of cohesion in the broadest

17

sense. To do so in a period when the implications of the Treaty on EU are already causing some political indigestion within the EC is particularly chancy. None of these considerations need necessarily be a bar to enlargement, but they do suggest that enlargement needs to be thought through by both those inside the EC and the aspirant members. Those inside have to contemplate what they may have to alter in their concept of Community integration. The aspirants need to think hard about what they would bring to the EC and what they would forgo by way of freedom of action, as well as what they hope to derive from it and in addition to the domestic problems that it might appear to alleviate. If the debate could be focused in this way, then the dialectics of enlargement could provide a new dynamic to the integration process.

1.5 Policy dilemmas
Much of the current debate about the adaptation of the EC to the next enlargement is focused on institutional issues, which are addressed in the next section. But there are real policy dilemmas to be faced as well, in particular:

1 Which established EC policies and activities might need to be refined or redefined?
2 Which new policy goals might be affected, positively or negatively?
3 Where should the lines be drawn in a larger EC between EC-level policy responsibilities and those exercised within the member states?
4 How wide a range of diversity of practice can or should be tolerated in a larger and more heterogeneous Community?
5 Which policy arenas might be left to other transnational organizations?

As regards the existing policies and established activities of the EC, two obvious areas stand out as demanding reappraisal: the common agricultural policy and the budget. Even to stretch the current CAP to the Eftans would be tricky, since with the partial exception of the Swedes the Eftans have expensive and protected agricultural policies. The arguments for CAP reform abound; here is yet another for proceeding promptly with the reform process, since it would be going backwards to add yet more clients of EC spending, who would in turn add barriers to reform. The geographical diversity of the EC would also increase: island states would be joined in their special pleading by mountainous, cold and sparsely populated states.

But if the case is strong as regards the Eftans, it is compelling as regards central and eastern Europe or any southern European candidates. The size of the agricultural sectors in the economies of many of these other potential candidates (relatively rather than in absolute volume, apart from Poland and Turkey) and the scope for modernization of their production methods make it necessary to contemplate more than marginal reforms of the CAP. But this issue arises not only in the context of enlargement, but also in the context of association. Liberalization of access to the EC's agricultural markets is necessary to make the Europe Agreements deliver results; it would be a prerequisite of an eastern or southeastern enlargement. Similar considerations apply to the so-called sensitive industrial sectors, such as textiles or steel.

A larger EC would also need a redesigned budget and pattern of expenditure policies and to look hard at how best to deal with the questions of cohesion and convergence. The Delors-2 proposals already and correctly begin to address these issues, though only up to a point since they concentrate for the moment on assumptions for the EC12. Somehow or other the sights of the existing members of the EC have to be lifted out of a debate about pork-barrel politics and side-payments towards an exploration of options for a different basis for resource allocation and fiscal transfers. Such a shift, however desirable, will be immensely difficult to negotiate and a zero-based EC budget would now have different starting-points. Yet some combination of value-for-money assessment and redefinition of transfer mechanisms would be valuable. In other words, a new MacDougal inquiry would be useful.

The Maastricht texts set important new policy goals for the EC: EMU, CFSP, with references to defence, and judicial cooperation. In the case of EMU, enlargement would bring in both the potential supporters of a full EMU from EFTA and in due course countries from elsewhere that would find the convergence targets very difficult indeed. The question which follows is whether enlargement would seriously complicate, or in some sense undermine, the EMU project. Any realistic answer to this has, however, to be based on a judgment about the prospects for EMU even among the EC12. If the EC is already prepared, as the Maastricht text suggests, to contemplate a final stage of EMU in which, for convergence reasons, not all 12 would immediately participate, then enlargement may not make all that much difference. Indeed the consequences of the September 1992 currency crisis may well make the EMU debate less relevant in practice to the enlargement debate, though the political backwash of the crisis should not be underestimated. A more immediate Eftan enlargement would perhaps introduce new members who would be keen to be in the inner circle. For the east Europeans, several prior steps would in any case be required to stabilize their economies and to proceed with the liberalization of capital markets.

Another important area will be the development of the social dimension. Even without the complication of the British 'opt-out' formula, enlargement would draw into the EC countries with very different kinds of social and welfare bases. The Eftans have traditionally high levels of welfare provision and social and employment standards, while the eastern and southern Europeans are faced with social adaptation and economic modernization. Some subtlety will therefore be required to strike a balance between such wide-ranging interests and concerns.

In the case of the CFSP, enlargement provokes two contrary impulses. First, for the neutral Eftans the issue is more to do with whether they can really accept the CFSP, or perhaps rather its potential development to underpin a common defence policy. Looked at from the EC side, the concern in several quarters is that in practice such countries might inhibit any such development.

Here the burden of proof will be placed on the applicants, who will be pressured to give very firm assurances that their various traditions of neutrality are not going to cause problems for the EC. Perhaps just willingness to sign the treaties will suffice; but perhaps applicants will be asked for an additional declaration. It should, however, be noted that the EC may be tempted to displace on to candidates issues that remain unresolved within the Twelve.

Second, for the east Europeans and Turkey the commitment to CFSP heightens their interest in full EC membership, as is clear from the Memorandum presented to the EC by the Visegrad Three in September 1992. From the EC side the questions will actually be much more about how far they are really prepared to see themselves as such close partners of the new democracies or Turkey, or to take on board what may as a consequence be some significantly different foreign and security policy priorities. This last point has so far been overshadowed by the discussion of neutrality. What may be much more important is to examine the new foreign policy preoccupations that new members would bring: for example, a long border with Russia and an important set of questions about Baltic security, or the considerable stake of Austria in working for Balkan stability. In addition there are very particularist questions as regards Malta's non-alignment and Libyan connections and the contested status of Cyprus. More broadly lies the question of whether a much larger EC could achieve sufficient cohesion and commonality of views to be an effective actor in foreign policy and eventually in the domain of defence as well. Here the issue of who can be or wants to be a member of WEU is also relevant.

Already the boundaries between the policy powers of the EC and those of its component members are contested. The debate ranges between what is held to be desirable, what can be legitimized by domestic publics and what is feasible or manageable on a collective basis. The Maastricht texts extended the scope for EC activities in a number of 'domestic' policy arenas – education, culture, public health and so on. Already the EC had become active in a number of areas where traditionally policies have been defined within countries on a much more parochial basis. The prospect of enlargement suggests that some lines will need to be drawn more firmly against this drift towards extending the policy scope of the EC. All the signs are that the political consequences of the ratification debates on Maastricht will lead to some retrenchment of Community ambitions. Some of this debate will in any case have to be played out as the EC grapples with the introduction of the concept of subsidiarity as a general principle governing Community policy-making. There may also be a case for thinking through which public goods can most usefully be pursued on a collective basis and which not.

The already heterogeneous EC of Twelve will become even more so with enlargement, however many members are taken in – heterogeneity of geography, history, politics, societies and economies. Behind the image of EC efforts to standardize and to make uniform lies already a different reality in which there is much experience of the differentiated application of EC policies and rules, sometimes in conception, more often in practical implementation. The single market programme has added to this by following the path of mutual recognition, which allows different rules to coexist within defined bands of tolerance and compatibility. On the face of it, enlargement seems to demand a willingness to work with and not against the grain of this heterogeneity, while still providing incentives to induce compatibility and convergence of practice. This issue was discussed somewhat *sub rosa* at the time of the SEA negotiations (prompted by the imminent accession of Spain and Portugal), but was hardly touched in the Maastricht IGC. It deserves to be addressed again. Last time round, the view that prevailed was in effect that differentiation (i.e. differentiated application of EC legislation, as distinct from subsidiarity, which is to do with the levels at which policy is made and implemented) should be accepted when there were compelling *objective* reasons for some divergence of rules and policy. The fisheries' issue for Iceland is a clear case in point, as might be Alpine transit. What is much more difficult to sustain without political and legal repercussions is arbitrary special pleading based on ephemeral political preferences. Variable geometry formulae are another route for accommodating diversity of capabilities and intensities of interest in particular spheres of collaboration.

A looming policy issue is what division of labour should be made with other European organizations. In the defence and security field the CFSP debate drew out some very different views on, for example, whether the aim should be eventually to merge WEU and the EC or to assign to each complementary tasks, with some kind of bridge between them. The debate on that will continue, with enlargement perhaps likely to induce some second and third thoughts, since the constellation of arguments might be different in an enlarged EC.

A different version of this debate has yet to take place over the respective roles of the EC and the Council of Europe, as the prospect begins to open up of most members of the Council of Europe moving towards EC membership. Perhaps the Council of Europe has a role to serve as a political antechamber, but if so perhaps that needs to be made explicit as a necessary but not sufficient condition of eventual EC membership. The human rights role of the Council of Europe is very important and may be better kept distinct from the EC, while providing a set of standards for the EC to judge how far an applicant has come in respect for human rights. The looser framework of the Council of Europe may turn out to be more appropriate for some arenas of policy, where either subsidiarity argues against disciplines as tight as those of the EC or where to bring them into the EC would add to the risk of over-loaded circuits. In addition the third pillar of the European Union touches areas of interest of the Council of Europe as regards judicial cooperation and home affairs, which are pertinent to some of the potential candidates for EC membership. All of these points imply a need for more explicit thinking about what kinds of policy the EC does best or better than the available alternatives.

All in all these policy dilemmas reveal the need for some thoughtful appraisal of EC policies, current and potential, and of how they might be most sensibly developed in a larger Community. In any case a mature political organization should be able to defend what it does well and to refrain from being trapped by what it has done less well or now might do differently. This suggests a need to interpret the *acquis communautaire* not stubbornly or rigidly, but with a degree of suppleness and sensitivity.

1.6 Institutional challenges

There is a kind of staleness in some of the debate about institutional issues in the EC, perhaps not surprisingly after the recent IGCs. There is also much over-simplification of the question of 'deepening' and political union. The Maastricht outcome, like previous EC conclaves on 'constitutional' issues, has left an ambiguity or tension between conditional transnationalism and firm supranationalism. Of course the enlargement debate cannot be divorced from this context, but enlargement also poses some different questions. One clear risk is that these may be reduced to a simple choice between the modification of the status quo and outright supranationalism. A second, perhaps equally great, risk is that the response to enlargement may be to make the institutional processes of the EC even more complicated, cumbersome and opaque than they are already.

So it is perhaps important to get down to basics as regards the institutional adaptations needed for a larger Community. Simply to enlarge the institutions in numerical proportions for new members will almost certainly not do. To add *pro rata* more Commissioners to a college that so many people consider to be already too unwieldy will serve no one's interests, nor would the kind of juggling performed in previous enlargements, whereby new recruits were brought into posts in the services by displacing current staff. To extend the number of MEPs on the current arbitrary proportions per member state will add little by way of enhanced democratic accountability. To factor new members automatically into the current voting rules and procedures of the Council could leave decision-making more vulnerable to eccentric vetoes and manipulative blocking minorities. Simply to lengthen the presidency rotation and the hazards of the alphabet will not help either to consolidate the pillars added by Maastricht or to facilitate partnership between the Council and the Commission. To retain

24

the segmented decision-making that permeates most of the institutions will not make the EC less prone to regulatory capture or more able to override those special interests that can mobilize at the EC level. These problems are not new, but enlargement exposes the costs of failing to tackle them.

One bottom-line requirement is surely that an enlarged EC will need a form of effective governance in the policy areas that are assigned to the EC level, its new pillars included. A second and increasingly important need is that this system of governance should be accepted as legitimate by the citizens of its members. The decisions facing a larger Community will be harder, not easier, to address. The range of factors to be taken into account will multiply. The need to be able to carry consent on difficult issues and to displace some vested interests will require persuasive political leadership and sensitive channels of political representation. Adroit technocratic manipulation behind closed doors, however benevolent and skilled, will not suffice.

So the institutions of a larger EC need to be *effective, legitimate and transparent*. Insiders need to know how to work the system and outsiders need to know what their points of access are. These basic points are probably much more important than a doctrinal debate about preferred approaches to political integration. But they also take the question of institutional adaptation on to ground where some hard choices have to be confronted and where there may be no soft options.

The criterion of enhanced effectiveness demands a tough assessment of the performance of *both* the Council *and* the Commission. As regards the *Council*, this implies action as regards decision rules, the segmentation that permits special interests to 'capture' particular policy arenas (agriculture is the prime but not the only example), and the presidency. Those who want the Council to remain the predominant organ have to follow through the logic and give it the capability to perform more incisively and to be held collectively to account for decisions taken and decisions avoided.

As for the *Commission*, whether or not it will emerge as a super-executive is a misleading phrasing of the question. Whether it will be given the tools to provide the engine of ideas and the fuel to deliver agreed policies seems much more important. At present the Commission is ludicrously under-resourced and over-constrained for its current tasks in an EC of Twelve. It is also too remote from accountable political responsibility to provide consistent policy leadership or to knock heads together in cases of stalled decision-making – the problems of the GATT round and CAP reform are apt examples. Thus there is a case for looking at how Commissioners are chosen, their links to the political transmission systems, the organization and staffing of the services and some experimentation with mechanisms of implementation. The debate about delegating tasks to special agencies, such as a Competition Office or regulatory bodies, may be given added boost by enlargement.

The *legitimacy* of the system depends partly on whether the Council and Commission are seen to be up to the tasks that they are assigned. Some of the post-Maastricht malaise suggests a lack of confidence on the part of the wider public, with consequential strains that could seriously handicap a larger Community. Part of the remedy lies beyond changes within the Council and the Commission and with parliaments, both European and national. A striking feature of the difficult debates in several member states over the Treaty on EU has been their introversion. Political parties, in spite of the much increased level of contact at the EC level, have not provided the transmission systems to sell the results of Maastricht or to substitute a definition of wider European concerns for the pull of parochialisms. But then the parties had made little direct input into the IGC process. They would need a bigger stake in the governance of the EC to bridge the continuing gap between national political debate and the European arena, to confer authority on the executive institutions, to intermediate between conflicting interests and to scrutinize decisions. In the absence of a bigger stake, the temptation – at both national and European levels – for parliamentarians to criticize and to trip up their executive branches will be powerful.

Here the EC may well have something to learn from the Nordic parliamentary traditions. The constant interaction between parliament and executive in the Nordic countries is very striking and has, after all, enabled some striking shifts of policy to take place, in Finland and Sweden at least. But enlargement would also bring into the EC countries in which governments are under tight scrutiny from both parliaments (the Swedes plan to copy the Danish Market Relations Committee) and publics (with direct democracy by referenda, Switzerland being the extreme case). These features are already intruding into the EC process from existing member states and will in any case need to be taken into account.

Greater *transparency* in the institutional system may be a requirement to achieve both improved effectiveness and more certain legitimacy. The EFTA countries that may join the EC are by and large endowed with rather open political systems and would arrive with expectations that full membership, unlike the opaque mechanisms of the EEA, would make the exercise of joint decision-making more accessible and more tangible. Recent trends in the EC have been in the opposite direction. Some of the proposals beginning to be floated for institutional modifications to take account of enlargement are strikingly arcane – one obvious example is the proposal for rotating troika presidencies in the Council.

Enlargement could bring into the EC not only more countries but more small countries: potentially Iceland and Liechtenstein among the Eftans; Malta and Cyprus; and from eastern Europe the Baltic states, the small republics of the former Yugoslavia and so on. Indeed only Poland and Turkey would count as larger members. This prospect has provoked considerable concern, both on general grounds and because of the implications for the Council presidency at a time when its role may increase as a manager of the CFSP. Hitherto the EC has dealt with the question of scale by a mix of parity principles (e.g. for the presidency) and weighting of influence (e.g. in voting rules), and by a combination of the two in nominations of Commissioners. Luxembourg is the only really small state among the current members. In past enlargements there were worries about whether the Irish or the Portuguese would be able to handle the presidency and about a single small state, e.g.

Greece, being able to block decisions taken under unanimity rules. Two forms of anxiety impinge in the debate: one is about 'micro-states'; and the other is about the 'under-representation' of the larger members in the EC system. Behind this debate also lurks the question of whether the really large states should be given even more weight in the system in some form of *directoire*.

So far the EC has avoided stirring the pot on these issues. There is deep resistance to the *directoire* concept. Small-country presidencies have not had such a bad track record and some large-country presidencies have been less than outstanding. The collegiality and sense of playing a respected part on quasi-equal terms has been an important element of 'solidarity' within the EC. Awkward small states have also served a purpose by strengthening the case for more majority voting (Andreas Papandreou's effect on Margaret Thatcher at the time of the SEA). The impact of individual Commissioners has been at least as much due to their qualities as individuals as to the kind of country from which they have come. There would have to be very good grounds for disturbing these useful conventions. So the question is whether enlargement provides such grounds. But the argument is up and running that the arrangements of the Council presidency should be reviewed, that who has the right to nominate a Commissioner should be re-examined, that voting weights in the Council need to be re-examined and that 'micro-states' might be offered less than full representation.

If there is a real problem, then there may be more than one way of dealing with it. Cumbersome formulae for designating groups of countries that would take turns in the presidency or to nominate a Commissioner, or for dividing up the tasks of the presidency are being canvassed, but need to be subjected to tough scrutiny as regards their costs as well as their benefits. Much of the problem would disappear if the EC had a more coherent and independent executive embedded in a framework of representative checks and balances and with a clear political legitimacy of its own.

1.7 Squaring the circle

Somehow or other the EC and its neighbours have to find a way through this maze. EC enlargement is going to remain in the middle of the European agenda for some time to come. So it would seem sensible to have an enlargement strategy and to follow it through: that is, to do precisely what did not happen with the EEA or the Europe Agreements, where interesting strategic concepts became denatured or degraded in various respects as they were negotiated. What then should be the basis of the strategy? First, not to confuse enlargement with partnership for privileged associates. Those would-be, but cannot-yet-be, members of the EC deserve more than a policy of rejection. Secondly, the EC needs to accept that the EC will be changed by enlargement and must concentrate on ensuring that the changes are for the better. If some of that hurts a bit, then the EC must find some pain-killers. Thirdly, the candidates need to think in multilateral terms and the overall interests and obligations of the EC, and not only in terms of their bilateral relations with the EC. Accession negotiations will work out better if there is seen to be an evenness of benefits and a mutual engagement of interests. Fourthly, the protagonists must avoid the temptation of Cartesianism. The real world of the EC12 is untidy and so will be the real world of a larger Community. Fifthly, the EC, important though it is, must not be seen as the be-all and end-all of European collaboration. Other organizations have roles to play and functions to fulfil. What is important is to be clear about those areas of policy and modes of collaboration where the EC has a good claim to primacy. Sixthly, everyone needs to come to the debate and the negotiations recognizing that some of the questions cannot be given routine answers.

The approach and assumptions set out above offer the chance of making some genuinely difficult issues more tractable. The probability is that there will be successive waves of enlargement. This means that those who will have to wait for later waves, in some cases perhaps for a very long time, also have to be engaged in substantive partnership. Thus the Europe Agreements with new democracies need quickly to be put on to a more generous footing, both politically and economically. It would also make very good sense for them to be given a multilateral character, by for example holding joint Association Councils or occasional joint summit meetings, both to start to engrain the patterns of coalition-building and mutual tolerance which have been so crucial in the EC's history and to prevent individual associates from being bilaterally squeezed by a Community that can always call more of the shots that any individual associate. And the EC perhaps needs to think more carefully *now* about whether the Europe Agreements are from here on more explicitly to be seen as the version of association for potential members or rather as an intensified version of a trade and cooperation agreement, which is exactly the question behind the Visegrad Memorandum. Meanwhile a better policy of substantive partnership needs to be found for those countries that lie on the boundaries of eligibility for full EC membership – Turkey now, Ukraine perhaps in due course.

Concepts need to be developed for EC membership that may not embrace every element of every pillar and may not be translated into identical results in every part of an enlarged Community. Whatever the terminology – differentiation, variable geometry, *abgestufte Integration* and so on – some experimentation will have to be done, otherwise enlargement will disappoint everyone. But it has to be done with care and must not confuse arbitrary subjectivity with objectively defined differences. Nor should any such debate be allowed to degenerate into slogans or mere rhetoric or the playing-out on the European stage of parochial domestic concerns. Would-be candidates are not interested in the slogans; they have real interests at stake in the political and economic substance.

All of this suggests that there should be an exploration of concepts alongside the more narrowly defined positioning of protagonists. The moment anyone with a vested interest in the outcome utters a remark on the options for reshaping an enlarged Community, motives become suspect. Hence the Commission was in a very difficult position in drafting the paper for the Lisbon European Council, as it will be in its follow-through. Equally the

British presidency needs to be sensitive to the charge that 'they would say that, wouldn't they?'.

So some brain-storming should be encouraged now to provoke ideas from those who have no vested interests as players in the process. Some open-minded questioning and reflection could be provoked by either the Council or the Commission or both, to accompany the accession negotiations and to contribute to preparations for the next IGC. Perhaps two kinds of brain-storming and outsider appraisal would be useful, termed here in shorthand – both the Monnet mode and the MacDougal mode. A MacDougal-type inquiry would involve a pooling of expertise on some of the substantive issues – the budget is an obvious case – where the tight positions of the players are inimical to fresh thinking or even cogent cost-benefit analyses. The Monnet mode implies some deliberate stretching of mind-sets and questioning of conventional wisdoms, but with a sharp eye on the practical problems that will still have to be solved at the end of the day.

2

The EC dimension

2.1 From European Community to European Union

The two intergovernmental conferences (IGCs), on Economic and Monetary Union (EMU) and European Political Union (EPU), were concluded in Maastricht in December 1991 after more than a year of intensive negotiations. There are divided opinions on the outcome of the summit as to how far the Treaty on European Union (EU) advances the EC on the path towards a new supranational structure. The member governments came to the negotiation table with different objectives reflecting their varied interests and domestic debates. The Treaty on EU is a complex document in which the differing interests of the member states have been accommodated and with new provisions to meet the challenge of external pressures crowding in on the EC.

The EU is built on three pillars. The first, the Community pillar, is rooted in the Treaties of Paris and Rome. The member states and the Community institutions together ensure that this pillar functions, and its scope has been extended. The second pillar consists of the common foreign and security activities of the EU. Its provisions are laid down in a framework of mainly intergovernmental cooperation, with the Commission associated and the European Parliament consulted. Justice and home affairs are to constitute the third pillar, also operating in an intergovernmental mode, with the institutions of the EC as yet having no real power of decision-taking within the third pillar.[1] Together these three pillars are to constitute the European Union, with the EC part by far the most extensive in scope and the consequential obligations for members the most specific and wide-ranging. The IGCs were convened for a mixture of purposes. The goal of the EMU had already been fairly clearly defined as the next logical phase of economic integration, leaving the IGC to negotiate on when and how to proceed to that goal. The second IGC, on EPU, was much less well prepared and was initially prompted by the event of German unification, to which became attached a number of proposals designed to strengthen the internal structures and thus deepen the Community by institutional reforms and introduce new areas of cooperation among the EC member states, as well as reinforce existing ones. The IGC did not have enlargement in its sights when it was convened, but it became increasingly clear that its implications for the achievability of political union were considerable.

Subsequently, as enlargement of the EC came on to the agenda, the European Council also laid down some broad principles on the widening of the Community in the conclusions of the Maastricht meeting. The Council noted that a number of European countries had submitted applications or announced their intentions to seek membership of the Union. The Commission was given the task of analysing the implications of enlargement of the EU and of presenting a report to the next European Council meeting in Lisbon.

The signing and ratification of the Treaty on EU will set the background for the candidate and potential candidate countries as regards the future membership negotiations. It should also be noted that the different debates about ratification in several member states will have some bearing on how the results and implications of Maastricht are interpreted in both existing and potential member states.

Eligibility
The Treaty on EU states in Article O that 'Any European State may apply to become a Member of the Union'. The conclusion of the European Council at Maastricht further referred to 'any European State whose systems of Governance are founded on the principle

of democracy may apply to become members of the Union'.[2] Article O does not, apart from the reference to 'the Union', amend Article 237 of the EEC (as amended by the Single European Act). When this was drawn up in 1957, Europe was divided; the eligible European countries were those to the southwest and the north, but not conceivably to the northeast, east or southeast, apart from Greece. Turkey was the only country whose European character became the subject of discussion because of its geographic position astride the border between Asia and Europe. On the other hand, the EC did not accept Morocco as an eligible candidate and, subsequently, did not officially consider the Moroccan application for EC membership. The point now has a new dimension, following the end of the artificial division between eastern and western Europe and the break-up of the Soviet Union. The definition of Europe has become elusive; after all, the Urals, which are normally regarded as the eastern frontier of Europe, have a distinct geographic location, but are not a frontier between states. Some of the components of the Confederation of Independent States (CIS) are European according to some definitions, such as parts of Russia and the Baltic states, while others are Asian. The European requirement might then be seen by any excluded candidates to be more political than geographical.

The principle of democracy is also an imprecise concept. It is not spelled out in the Treaties. At the time of Mediterranean enlargement the Council of Ministers debated whether to entrench a definition of democracy, but could only agree on a declaration. It is clear from the Community side that the underlying assumption is a democratic system according to western values. Democratic states would be those which organize free and just elections, practise the rule of law and show respect for civil and human rights. In Article F of the Treaty on EU, the importance of systems of government founded on principles of democracy and respect for fundamental rights is underlined for the first time as an express Treaty commitment. The responsibility for evaluating how far this principle is respected might in effect be assigned to the European Parliament, which has a decisive power of veto through the procedure of codecision on enlargement. Membership of the Council of Europe and the UN (because of Community activities in foreign policy) might become prerequisites for any candidate country to be considered.

But, a potentially eligible candidate has in practice other conditions to fulfil. The country must have developed a stable market economy based on private entrepreneurship and a well-functioning financial sector. Since the agreement on the EMU and the development towards a single European currency, it is clear that several potential candidates could not meet either the requirements of full capital liberalization or conditions of convergence. How far a willingness to accept or to fulfil the latter is a prerequisite of EC membership in itself is not clear. However, those current member governments which favour a swift transition to the final stage of the EMU might be reluctant to accept a candidate which had not experienced a high and sustainable level of economic growth during the period preceding the accession, let alone to contemplate the resource transfers which might be implied.

Finally, the acceptance of the *acquis communautaire* (see below) is a fundamental condition of membership. By agreeing on the Treaty on EU, the Community took yet another step towards integration. It seems probable that future candidates will have to prove their political commitment to the ultimate goals, or *finalités politiques*, of the Union. In this context, the state of public opinion within a candidate country might be considered relevant. It could be a decisive hurdle to entry, if large and important groups in the society were strongly against membership, and those negotiating accession would have difficulties in convincing the Community that their country was prepared for membership.

The acquis communautaire

The *acquis communautaire* could well be described as being something that 'everybody has heard about it, but nobody knows what it looks like'. The reason for the confusion about its exact definition is that practitioners and academics use the term differently in different contexts. There have been attempts to translate it into

English, but the result thus far is only the unsatisfactory 'Community patrimony' or 'Community heritage'. The French term has prevailed and become increasingly embedded.

The *acquis communautaire* is composed of the treaties of the EC and the regulations, directives, decisions and recommendations derived from them, as well as the case law from the European Court of Justice (ECJ). It comprises the policies, the legal framework and the institutional structure which a country must accept. The principle of the acceptance of the *acquis communautaire* was first mentioned in the context of the first enlargement of the EC. France was for a long time reluctant to accept the consequences for the overall balance of the Community brought about by the accession of the UK, a big country that traditionally had strong ties with other parts of the world, and some very different policies. The UK, it was argued, would bring in a different set of ideas that threatened to dilute the European integration process and to endanger the existence of the Community. The French were finally persuaded to change position, but only after having stated as a condition of entry the principle of total acceptance of the *acquis communautaire*. The negotiations that followed dealt exclusively with transitional measures and terms of adaptation. The acceptance of the *acquis communautaire* remained a precondition in the second and third enlargements, as well as in the limited negotiations with the EFTA countries to set up the EEA. The principle has made the EC appear as a tough and unyielding negotiating partner, and several acceding countries have carried with them into the Community a feeling of having been accorded onerous terms of entry or having paid too high a price.

The insistence on keeping the *acquis communautaire* intact explains in part the inflexibility of the Community system, but hints also at an additional dimension of the EC. When acceding, a candidate has to show commitment to the principles, goals, norms and values of the Community. The EC is said to 'rest upon an implicit contract, in that its member states accept mutual obligations in return for mutual benefits. Continued respect for that contract requires a sense in all member states not only that the costs and benefits of membership are distributed equitably, but also that the rules and obligations which each has accepted are accepted and observed by all.'[3]

The fear of free-riders explains why acceding countries are made to accept the rules of the game by taking on board the *acquis communautaire* at the time of accession to the Community structure.

This notion of the *acquis communautaire* became a widely cited principle, but until recently had been mentioned in the rulings of the ECJ and negotiators' parlance, but not in the treaties of the EC. In Articles B and C of the common provisions, the European Union, however, sets itself the following objective:

> to maintain in full the *acquis communautaire*, and build on it with a view to considering ... to what extent the policies and forms of cooperation introduced by this Treaty may need to be revised with the aim of ensuring the effectiveness of the mechanisms and the Institutions of the Community. The Union shall be served by a single institutional framework which shall ensure the consistency and the continuity of the activities carried out in order to attain its objective while respecting and building upon the *acquis communautaire*.

The provisions make the *acquis communautaire* a term of art in the Treaties and give it an additional weight. The barrier to membership has been raised in order to ensure homogeneity and so as to promote deepening of the Community in parallel with the process of widening. It can also be interpreted as a warning flag to candidate countries of tough negotiations to come: both to the group of countries which will have problems in adapting to the *acquis communautaire* of the EMU and the internal market; and to the group of countries which have no major technical or economical problems, but where there are worries about loss of sovereignty and doubts about the ultimate goals of the Union, for example, a common defence policy.

The importance of the *acquis communautaire* in the context of enlargement was stressed in the Commission's report. The Commission defined the *acquis* as:

the contents, principles and political objectives of the Treaties, including the Maastricht Treaty; the legislation adopted in implementation of the Treaties, and the jurisprudence of the Court; the declarations and resolutions adopted in the Community framework; the international agreements, and the agreements between member states connected with the Community's activities.

The Common Foreign and Security Policy

The European Union has now endowed itself with a common foreign and security policy (CFSP), which will be implemented through intergovernmental procedures. The member states will still be free to act in areas where the Union has not yet taken any decision, but on issues of joint action, as defined by the Treaty, the Council of Ministers' decisions will be binding. Three areas of joint action have been mentioned thus far: the CSCE process; disarmament, control of armaments in Europe and non-proliferation; and economic aspects of security. Provisions have been made for the possible addition of new areas of cooperation. The Union has not yet acquired a common defence policy, but the intention to make Western European Union (WEU) the defence component of the Union is stated.

The CFSP will, once the Treaty is ratified, become a part of the *acquis politique*, another much-used phrase which defies exact definition. It implies that potential candidate countries will have to comply with this regime of the Union, adopt its shared policies and implement any decisions taken in its framework. When it comes to the development of a common defence policy, this could create a difficult situation for those EFTA countries which have so far maintained their various policies of neutrality. How far they will continue to redefine their concepts of neutrality will to a certain extent be a matter of internal debate, but undoubtedly the Community would like to see clear signs of commitment to the CFSP and have guarantees of their solidarity with joint actions of the Union. Some member countries fear that an additional number of neutrals might dilute future developments in defence matters of the Union, and slow down the progress towards common defence policy in the next IGC, scheduled for 1996. There is a direct link between the Union's *acquis politique* and a potential candidate's membership of organizations which already operate in areas defined as appropriate for joint action. The Union will play an important role in building an all-European security order within the framework of the CSCE.

A declaration is attached to the Treaty on behalf of existing members of WEU, whereby they reassert their goals of developing a European security and defence identity, expanding the role of WEU and, in the longer term, pursuing a common defence policy, all to be compatible with the Atlantic Alliance. In a second section of the declaration, the current WEU members invite the other European members of the European Union to join WEU, and offer other European members of NATO the opportunity to become associate members.

In June 1992, the Italian presidency of WEU opened talks on enlargement. So far, of the current EC member states only Greece has asked for full membership; Ireland is considering observer status; and Denmark has not made any approach to WEU on this matter, but took part in the meeting. Of the European NATO countries not (yet) members of the EC, Turkey has asked for full membership, while Norway and Iceland have expressed interest in becoming associate members. A timetable for enlargement negotiations aims at reaching their conclusion by the end of 1992.[4]

The foreign and defence ministers of WEU met their opposite numbers from Bulgaria, the Czech and Slovak Federal Republic (CSFR), Estonia, Hungary, Latvia, Lithuania, Poland and Romania on 19 June 1992, in Petersberg near Bonn. The ministers decided that: 'The enhancement of WEU's relations with Bulgaria, Czech and Slovak Republic, Estonia, Hungary, Latvia, Lithuania, Poland and Romania should reflect their specific relations which exist and are developing between these countries and the European Union and its member states.'[5] The statement makes it clear that the integration process between the central and east European countries and the WEU will follow the development of the relations with the Community. The General Secretary of the WEU, Willem van Eekelen, confirmed this as follows: 'Central European countries which have – or will shortly have – association links with the Community may be parties to thinking on the conditions of European security. At the same time the links with the EC could be used as a criterion to determine with whom we should form a special relationship.'[6]

The principle of subsidiarity

The Treaty on EU lays down the basic principle of subsidiarity. Article 3b states that

> in the areas which do not fall within its exclusive competence, the Community shall take action, in accordance with the principle of subsidiarity, only if and in so far as the objectives of the proposed action cannot be sufficiently achieved by the Member States and can therefore ... be better achieved by the Community.

This principle will become increasingly important in an enlarged Community.[7] President Delors has on several occasions stated that it is crucial for the future development of the Union that subsidiarity become the guiding principle of the activities of the EC institutions. As the number of the member states grows, the subsidiarity approach should permit an efficient sharing of law and decision-making power between different levels of government and continued regional characteristics. As the Union develops its institutions and structures, for Delors and for many others necessarily along federal lines, subsidiarity could solve a number of issues concerning the role and competences of regions vis-à-vis the national administrations and the EC, as well as the division of powers in fiscal and economic policy questions, for example as regards the rights to impose taxes, management of structural funds, etc.

The Community is currently engaged in a discussion on how to define subsidiarity more closely and its practical implications. The texts of the Treaty are not entirely clear and the scope of the principle remains to be decided by the member states, by the

Community institutions and ultimately by the ECJ. Several legal experts, including some from the ECJ, had already commented before the European Council meeting in Maastricht that subsidiarity was 'political in essence' and not legal; thus, the European Council would be the judge of last resort.[8]

Jacques Delors is a long-standing proponent of the principle of subsidiarity as a vital component in the EU. After the Danish vote against the Treaty on EU, influenced partly by controversy about plans attributed to the President of the Commission to increase the executive power of the Commission in an enlarged Union, he committed himself to building a more open Community and more transparent decision-making procedures within the EC institutions and with decisions to be taken according to the principle of subsidiarity. At the European Council in Lisbon in June 1992, he presented some ideas on how the Commission might implement subsidiarity in its work in the future. To Delors, subsidiarity means taking decisions as close to the citizens as possible and in conditions offering the greatest efficiency. Thus, at municipal, regional and state level, but also inversely at Community level if Community action is essential. At the Lisbon meeting, Jacques Delors made two proposals: first, that the Commission should in all new proposals justify the reasons for which action was needed at the Community level; and, second, that the Commission was prepared to re-examine existing legislation, so as to adapt it to the principle of subsidiarity.[9]

Denmark and the UK have stressed the principle of subsidiarity as a means to make the Union more attractive to their populations and parliaments. Indeed in both countries it has been argued that some further elaboration of the Maastricht text should be made quickly so as to permit ratification to proceed. The German government also entered the debate to support the clarification of subsidiarity, prompted in part by concerns at the Länder level. In the short term any new language could be only declaratory, though the debate is already influencing behaviour in the EC. Over the longer term it may well be that new legal texts will be agreed which might both alter the scope of Community powers and leave individual members more freedom of action on specific policy issues. Whatever the outcome, the debate on subsidiarity will have a crucial bearing on the future shape of the EC.

For the potential candidate countries, the principle of subsidiarity is also attractive. Switzerland in particular has welcomed this new approach, arguing that subsidiarity suits the Swiss federal system well, and therefore that its systematic operation could make easier the choice as to whether to join the Community. It has even been suggested that in the area of CFSP, the principle of subsidiarity might be useful for any applicant countries which could not participate fully in all provisions, especially as regards an eventual defence policy. However, neither the principle nor the practice of subsidiarity is sufficiently defined to provide political and legal guidance on how a larger and more diverse Community would operate.

Social and economic cohesion

A new issue for the EC, as it has enlarged, has been how to handle disparities of wealth and economic performance among its members. Cohesion was first written into Community texts in the Single European Act and translated into practice in the Delors package of 1988 on the budget. It was further developed when Spain, together with the other Mediterranean countries and Ireland, succeeded in securing a commitment of larger financial support from richer member countries at the Maastricht European Council. A new cohesion fund is to be established with the objective of ensuring economic and social cohesion in the Community by supporting projects necessary to reach EC standards in the areas of environment and infrastructure. The Spanish government argued that, in the absence of extra financial transfers, the poorer member states would have to divert money to these areas when the overriding priority ought to be compliance with the convergence criteria of EMU. An additional attempt to strengthen financial solidarity in the EC was laid down in the agreement in principle on new guidelines for budgetary contributions that would take a country's relative wealth into consideration. This principle could address some of the distortions created by the CAP, in that cohesion and progressive resource transfers would benefit the southern member states at the expense of those northern states whose agricultural sectors traditionally are favoured by the CAP. This is, however, to beg a question about CAP reform and another about net payers to, and net beneficiaries of, EC funding.

The enlargement of the Community will have two implications for the principle of cohesion. In the case of the accession of EFTA countries, the 'rich north' would be strengthened. The demands for internal transfers of money to poorer members would increase, as all the EFTA countries are expected to become net contributors. The EFTA states showed their preparedness to contribute to the financial solidarity of the Community already during the EEA negotiations, when they agreed to set up an EEA cohesion fund for the benefit of the southern EC member states and Ireland. It should be pointed out that their contributions can never be large in absolute terms, in that the size of their combined GNP is approximately ten times smaller than that of the EC12.[10] Once the Eftans are inside the EC, they might be eligible themselves for some support from EC structural funds, to take into account certain special features of the candidates (e.g. Arctic agriculture), but they would on the whole not compete for funds. In the case of Hungary, the CSFR and Poland (or other east European countries) becoming members of the EC, the situation would be essentially different. They would be eligible on current criteria for substantial financial transfers from the structural funds, and pressures would be strong to extend the cohesion funds to the eastern candidates. Their economic output is heavily based on agriculture (the CSFR less so), and agricultural employment is considerably higher than in the EC. Under the CAP system, if it remained as today, they would enjoy high guaranteed prices, but would have to comply with the quota restrictions. Were the CAP to move towards an income support system, the costs implied by financial solidarity would also be substantial. The same would be true in the case of the accession of Turkey. The financial impact of the entry of Cyprus and Malta would be negligible because of the small size of their economies; though both are agricultural producers, Mediterranean products are less heavily supported by the CAP.

In the light of this scenario, it has to be assumed that to extend 'budgetary solidarity' to Turkey and the newly established market economies in central and eastern Europe would be to run into difficulties, since already contested resources would have to be shared among more members in a further enlarged Community. The veto of some countries could 'hang in the air' during the accession negotiations, as existing budget beneficiaries sought 'compensation' for potential financial losses as a result of enlargement.

The real cost of enlargement could be estimated only after a new budgetary approach has been agreed on, revising the criteria for financial contributions and eligibility. The negotiations on the Delors-2 package, currently under way, are intended to prepare for reform. But this package is already causing considerable controversy within the Community.

The Maastricht European Council noted that negotiations on accession to the European Union can start as soon as the Community has terminated its negotiations on own resources and related issues. The preliminary negotiations are already proving to be thorny: the largest net contributor, Germany, has stressed the burden on the German economy and society brought about by the considerable sums being transferred to the five new Länder. Some member countries, notably Denmark, Italy and the Netherlands, have shown themselves unwilling to move to a new financial basis for relating budget contributions to national economic performance. They are all net contributors under the current system. Others, especially the UK and Germany, question the necessity of increasing the ceiling of the budget in order to reach the objectives of the EU Treaty. Since the negotiations on the Delors-2 package are running in parallel to the ratification process of the Treaty on EU, many issues that touch national sensitivities are being raised and it cannot be presumed that agreement on Delors-2 will quickly be achieved.

Opting-in and opting-out

Each time the EC has been enlarged there has been a debate about how far all member states could or would accept the same level of engagement in all areas of EC policy and legislation. Terms such as 'variable geometry', *'abgestufte Integration'*, 'differentiation' and 'two-speed' have been coined to highlight the possible consequences of partial engagement in particular policies. The Maastricht agreement added two new elements to the debate, as regards EMU and on social policy.

Already the 1979 agreement on the European Monetary System (EMS) recognized that not all member states would necessarily participate fully from the outset. Since then, countries applying less stringently the provisions of the exchange-rate mechanism have narrowed their bands, while others applying only parts of the EMS now participate in the whole operation. The same issue arose in the recent EMU negotiations, in two distinct forms. Some governments, notably Britain (less visibly Denmark), wanted to reserve the final political decision on participation in the third phase until later, hence the protocols in the Treaty on EU agreed that 'the United Kingdom shall not be obliged or committed to move to the third stage of Economic and Monetary Union without a separate decision to do so by its government and Parliament,' and that 'the Danish Constitution contains provisions which may imply a referendum in Denmark prior to Danish participation in the third stage of Economic and Monetary Union'. But, in addition, those who wanted EMU to go ahead wanted to be sure that they would be able to impose tough convergence criteria on the lagging economies of some members. Consequently, the EMU text sets both conditions and a quorum to be achieved for the decision in 1997 or 1999 to move to a single currency. As a result, it is widely assumed that not all member states will move together to a single currency at the end of the decade. Quite how these rules would be applied to new members remains to be seen.

The outcome on the 'social chapter' is very different. There was a strong opposition from the UK to the proposed chapter on social policy in the Maastricht draft text. The other 11 member countries decided to proceed with further integration among themselves, and agreed on a special protocol to enable them to follow EC procedures extraordinarily and to define the Social Charter as a part of the *acquis communautaire*. Legally, this new dimension is not yet an integral part of the EC treaties, and its status as a part of the *acquis communautaire* is being discussed.[11] It remains to be seen whether acceding countries will have to accept these additional elements of social policy as an integral part of the Community framework. With their generally high national standards, EFTA applicants are unlikely to see this as a problem.

The practical consequences of the arrangement between the UK and the other 11 member states have given rise to a renewed discussion of a 'two-speed' Europe or a Europe of 'two tiers'.[12] The declaration on social policy states that the UK 'shall not take part in deliberation and the adoption by the Council of Commission proposals made on the basis of the Protocol' (in the social area). Opinions vary on the extent to which this arrangement is a loosening-up of the Community framework or if it will speed up integration between other member countries.

In an enlarged Community, it is possible to foresee a core of well-integrated countries pushing integration further among themselves, but outside the framework of the treaties of the EC. The EFTA applicants would certainly have an interest in higher standards, for example in the social field, and would be obvious candidates for full participation in the third phase of the EMU. However, for Turkey and the central and east European countries, higher standards might handicap their chances of catching up economically with the Community. They would also find onerous the constraints and convergence criteria of EMU.

2.2 Community attitudes to enlargement[13]

The European Council stated in the conclusions of the Maastricht summit that negotiations on the next phase of enlargement 'can start as soon as the Community has terminated its negotiations on own resources and related matters in 1992' and that 'a number of European countries have submitted their applications or announced their intention of seeking membership of the Union'. This statement was in itself a compromise, as some member governments had wanted to mention explicitly the two EFTA countries, Austria and Sweden, which had already presented their applications. The careful wording of the clause left the field open to the Community to decide on the context, the circumstances and the candidates with which membership negotiations would begin.

The European Council at Maastricht invited the Commission to examine the implications for the Community of enlargement and to present its conclusions to the Lisbon European Council in June 1992. The Commission set up a task force to draft a report and it was careful not to take an official position on the question until this work was completed.

The Lisbon European Council and enlargement
The Commission's report, presented to the European Council in Lisbon on 26–27 June 1992, formed the basis of the EC leaders' discussion of enlargement. The Conclusions of the Presidency set out an approach to enlargement of the Community, with some qualifications as regards the candidate countries and with some conditions which would have to be fulfilled before accession negotiations can start. The European Council reaffirmed its objective of remaining open to 'any European States whose system of government is founded on the principle of democracy ... that aspire to full participation (of the Union) and who fulfil the conditions for membership' and agreed that 'negotiations on accession to the Union on the basis of the Treaty agreed in Maastricht can start as soon as the Community has terminated its negotiations on Own Resources and related issues in 1992'.

The statement made clear that the accession of new members would be based on the provisions of the Treaty on EU and that countries would be treated as applicants for membership of the Union. So the first prerequisite for negotiations to start is that the Treaty on EU has to be ratified. The turmoil in several member states over ratification has created some confusion as to what is to be taken as the *acquis* and has hence left some doubts as to the basis of negotiations. Several political leaders have insisted that opt-out clauses, protocols and declarations attached to the Treaty would be applicable *only* to the existing member that is explicitly mentioned. If Denmark were to be granted a special status in certain areas deemed especially sensitive, such as the common defence policy as well as the third stage of the EMU, on which there is already a Danish declaration, the *acquis* of the Union would no longer be so clear-cut. Applicant countries might be asked to comply more stringently than certain existing members with provisions of the Treaties that are contested.

The Lisbon European Council reaffirmed as a second prerequisite for negotiations the conclusion of the negotiations on the Delors-2 package and related issues. The Delors-2 package is directly linked to the ratification of the Treaty on EU, with its provision on the establishment of a cohesion fund, but also affects the revenue burden for the member states. This point is especially important for the applicant EFTA states, since they are generally expected to become net contributors. The five-year package will become part of the *acquis*.

The Lisbon European Council nevertheless gave the go-head (subject to the conditions above) for early negotiations with those EFTA countries which have, or will have, applied for membership before the negotiations start. It invited 'the institutions to speed up with the preparatory work needed to ensure rapid progress including the preparation before the European Council in Edinburgh of the Union's general negotiation framework'. The Commission issued its Opinion on Sweden in July 1992, with those on Finland due in late 1992 and on Switzerland in late 1992 or early 1993. If Norway applies, it may be possible to produce an opinion fairly quickly by updating the one from the early 1970s.

The statement of the European Council referred to *official* negotiations, perhaps implying that unofficial negotiations could start already under the British presidency. It had been thought that the official accession negotiations could be opened early in 1993, but this has become less certain in the different light of the delays over Maastricht, to the irritation of the more impatient enlargers.

It is, however, possible that preparations at the technical level could cover enough ground to permit official negotiations to be concluded speedily. Austria, Sweden, Finland and Switzerland might still achieve their objective of becoming members before the next IGC, scheduled for 1996.

The final remark of the European Council concerning the EFTA applicants was that 'this enlargement is possible on the basis of the institutional provisions contained in the Treaty on the Union and attached declarations'. Basically, this implies that the member states accepted enlargement to EFTA countries before the next IGC and thus ahead of a major reform of the institutions. This would not necessarily be the case for other applicants declared or potential.

The wider responsibilities of an enlarged Union towards other candidates for membership or countries that have close links to the Union were also acknowledged. The European Council stressed the increasingly important role of Turkey, advocating that relations should be developed beyond the Association Agreement of 1963 to include a political dialogue at the highest level. The signal to Turkey was that, although early full membership may not be possible, the member states were eager to promote close relations with the Turks. This political dimension is reflected in the invitation to association with WEU and intensified cooperation within the framework of NATO.

As for Malta and Cyprus, the European Council had little to add to the Commission's report, which did not envisage their early accession.

The last section of the Presidency Conclusions was devoted to the central and east European countries. The European Council reaffirmed 'the Community's will to develop its partnership with these countries within the framework of the Europe Agreements in their efforts to restructure their economies and institutions'. The European Council promised to intensify and extend the political dialogue and that 'cooperation will be focused systematically on assisting their efforts to prepare the accession to the Union which they seek'.

The context of accession negotiations

Before dealing with the range of opinions on enlargement held by the member states and the Commission, it is important to map out the context in which accession negotiations would take place and the conditions of entry which the candidate countries will have to meet. The framework of negotiations has recently become more complex.

The basis for any accession negotiations is the *acquis communautaire* and *politique*, as extended by the Treaty on EU, assuming that the Treaty concluded in Maastricht will be ratified by the member states in one way or another. Views differ on how far the candidates will be asked to give guarantees that they endorse the *finalités politiques* (or ultimate political goals) of the Union, but the underlying principle is clearly underlined in the Treaty in the explicit mention of the *acquis communautaire* (see section 2.1). It is widely asserted by the member states and inside the EC institutions that the opt-out clause as regards the social chapter in the Treaty on EU is to be applied solely to the UK. There would be strong opposition to its being deemed a precedent for candidate countries wanting to obtain similar provisions in a policy area covered by the EU. The UK arrangement, however, makes it harder to assess what the *acquis* will comprise in the social area. Nevertheless, the fact that the texts of the treaty are in some senses deliberately ambiguous will lead to a discussion as to their interpretation, and different philosophies about the goal of integration will come to the fore. The neutral EFTA countries might run into difficulties in trying to convince the EC of their 'solidarity' with Community actions of a security and military nature. Many people believe that, as long as discussions are kept pragmatic, it will be possible to find a solution at this point. But, if any EC member state wants to complicate the negotiations, there is scope for defining neutrality as a problem.

Economic and social solidarity among the EC member states is spelled out in the treaty through the objective of economic convergence crucial to the success of the EMU. The gradual achievement of EMU has been agreed to require a higher degree of economic and social cohesion, which is to be achieved through financial transfers from richer to poorer member states. The Delors-2 budget proposal paves the way for achieving this by raising budget revenue from 1.2% to 1.37%, later revised to 1.34%, of the total GNP of the EC, and by readjusting the contribution system to reflect better the performance of member states' economies. The proposal has been heavily criticized by several member states. Some question the necessity of raising the budget ceiling, in that a general increase in economic output would generate sufficient extra funding, though in a period of recession this might be limited. Others doubt the fairness of granting cohesion money to explicitly designated countries, when there are other regions in the Community that are arguably way behind the Community average in economic development. Yet another group complains about the new system of determining national contributions to the Community budget, since it would change their status from net receivers to contributors.

The Lisbon European Council gave some guidelines for the EcoFin Council's negotiations on the future financing of the Community. It confirmed the agreement reached in the framework of the CAP and that enough financial means should be provided for to guarantee farmers' incomes. The principle of economic and social cohesion represents an essential dimension of the Community, and the Cohesion Fund, as agreed in the Treaty on EU, for member states with a GNP representing less than 90% of average Community GNP is to be established. Equivalent treatment will also have to be granted the five new German Länder. Finally, the European Council confirmed that measures had to be taken to correct the regressive nature of the current financing system. The position taken by the European Council was confirmed by the finance ministers in August 1992, who reaffirmed the commitments made at Lisbon and Maastricht.

With the prospect of a continuing difficult economic climate, some member states have started to question the extent of the principle of economic solidarity in the Community and the consequent liabilities. Were the Community in the future to enlarge to countries that would claim substantial financial transfers, the pressures on the budget would increase from both internal and external claimants (in the former Soviet Union, eastern Europe or the Mediterranean basin). There is an emerging discussion about the need for a major restructuring of the budget system and the CAP before an enlargement to the east or the south could take place.

In the short term, however, the provisions for financial support in the Delors package are linked to the question of enlargement, a fact that is recurrently stressed by the beneficiary member countries. The link, explicitly stated by the Lisbon European Council, will become an important argument in decision-making about the start of membership negotiations. The financially reticent states (most notably Germany and the UK) are positive as regards an early enlargement, and wave a warning flag of difficult and prolonged endorsement processes by their national parliaments if the contributions to the budget were to increase too much. Some people think that the budget settlement could be achieved only by bringing in a larger number of net contributors so as to ease the financial burden of the few current net payers.

The Delors-2 package also deals with the difficult subject of agricultural reform, already on the agenda with the MacSharry proposals. The Commission wants to reduce further the proportion of the sums spent on agriculture and to transfer the liberated resources to structural funds and research. The member states accepted that agricultural reform had to be pushed further in order to resolve the deadlock with the USA in the GATT negotiations. Agricultural ministers had agreed to endorse the MacSharry proposal on 21 May 1992 after long and difficult negotiations. The deal is intended to reduce the Community's food mountains and eventually lead to lower consumer prices. Whether this will be enough to break the deadlock remains to be seen. Hopes for a softening of the French position were checked by the outcome of the French referendum on Maastricht in which the anti-EC sentiments within the farming community were evident.

Although the European Council in Lisbon concluded that the first wave of enlargement with EFTA applicants could take place within the existing institutional framework, there are diverging opinions among the member states as to the timing of enlargement in relation to the next IGC in 1996, originally planned to look at the evolution of the CFSP. In previous enlargements of the Community, deepening has accompanied widening. The accession negotiations with Spain and Portugal took place in parallel with a reform process that led to the Single European Act. Indeed it was originally because of imminent enlargement that the Dooge committee was set up in 1984 and the 1985 IGC convened. The Portuguese and Spanish were associated with its later stages. Measures to improve the efficiency of the EC institutions were adopted by increasing the competences of the Commission in the implementation process of Community policies, increased decision-making power for the European Parliament and an extension of qualified majority voting in the Council in matters covered by the internal market programme.

In the run-up to the fourth enlargement, some believe that deepening is a prerequisite for widening and would like the next IGC to take place before the accession of new members. Others argue that the debate on institutional reform should be held in 1996, with the new member countries taking part. However, the turmoil over the ratification of the Treaty on EU, and the lack of preparedness of EC citizens to endorse further integration, now makes radical changes harder to envisage.

The views of current EC members
The statements from the European Council in Lisbon imply that the member states have all accepted the inevitability of enlargement. Even though not all EC governments are enthusiastic at the prospect, there is a consensus that the prosperous economies and politically stable societies of the EFTA states would have a beneficial impact on the EC. It had initially been widely assumed that the next phase would be an enlargement limited to Austria, Sweden and Finland. The Swiss application has thrown this into question. The debate in Norway could well produce a membership application in November. Iceland and Liechtenstein have not yet stated the intention to seek membership, but they watch closely develop-

ments in the other EFTA countries. If only Iceland and Liechtenstein remained in EFTA, it is difficult to foresee how the EEA decision-making process would in practice function satisfactorily and the two countries would be ludicrously isolated.

The consensus, confirmed by the Lisbon European Council, is that it will take the central and east European countries much longer to prepare for full EC membership. The Portuguese presidency quoted Portugal's accession as an example of a long and demanding process of adaptation to EC membership. Some member countries which are sceptical as regards an eastern enlargement argue that the state of their economies, as well as the lack of experience of societies based on market economy and democratic principles, would make these countries vulnerable to competition inside the EC and reduce them to economic satellites. This group of member states, which includes France, Italy, Spain and Portugal, have adopted a 'wait-and-see' approach, leaving the Europe Agreements to prepare the countries economically and politically for membership. But, if account is taken of the severe criticism made in several quarter of the Europe Agreements (see section 4.2), this formula of association might not be an adequate model for the gradual integration of these countries into the Community. Conversely, Germany and the UK would like to see Poland, Hungary and the CSFR more closely integrated with the EC as soon as possible, both for security and stability reasons and because economic restructuring could be faster and more efficient if they were inside the EC framework. In both cases the language of politicians implies that soon means very soon, while officials tend to speak in a more medium-term perspective. However, the Lisbon European Council stressed the importance of intensifying partnership with the east Europeans, irrespective of their eventual chances of EC accession, a point which echoed the Commission's report.

Bulgaria and Romania are now negotiating Europe Agreements with the Community. The foreign ministers have expressed hopes that the accords will be ready to sign as soon as possible, but the exact timetable is not yet clear; Bulgaria will very probably sign before Romania. In due course, similar agreements will be negotiated with Slovenia, Croatia, perhaps other parts of the former Yugoslavia, Albania and the Baltic states, but the logical prior step is a trade and cooperation agreement. So far, cooperation agreements have been signed with the Baltic states and Albania. In July 1992, the Commission was granted a mandate to start to negotiate a cooperation agreement with Slovenia.

The southern European countries are by and large considered to raise economic, social, administrative or political problems which suggest that accession is not yet appropriate. Malta is increasingly seen as a special case, although opinions differ as to whether or not Maltese membership is a problem for the Community's institutional balance, given its small size. The question which is asked is whether Malta and Cyprus would be able to assume the full institutional responsibility of membership – i.e. to take on the role of the presidency of the Council and have a Commissioner – or whether they should be offered a 'special status' without these rights and obligations. Whether the EC could decide to offer Malta and Cyprus such a status would partly depend on the position taken by Luxembourg, which does not share the view that the size of a country need be a hurdle to its effective participation in the Community machinery. It remains to be seen whether Malta and Cyprus could accept a 'special status' agreement, or whether a compromise could be found with Luxembourg, to let it retain a 'normal status' on the basis of its position as a founding member and its experience in Community affairs. Other smaller EC members could be drawn into any such debate to judge by reactions from, e.g., the Danes and the Dutch to proposals in this vein. Significant in this context is the Memorandum from the three Benelux countries tabled at the European Council in Lisbon. This stressed that enlargement of the Union would have 'important implications, especially for the smaller countries, since they:

- may change, more than in the past, the nature and form of the Community;
- might cause, from the point of view of the founder countries, fundamental distortions in the basic objectives to which they are still attached; and

- may erode the position and role of the smaller member countries.'[14]

The southern member states are more favourable to Maltese accession, and Spain favours membership negotiations with Malta in parallel to those with the EFTA states. EC governments so far have regarded the Cyprus application as blocked by the partition of the island because of the dispute with Turkey. By far the most difficult case is Turkey, which as long ago as 1963 was offered the prospect of membership. EC governments would, by and large, prefer the Turkish application to go away. Recent events have shown that some EC member countries are willing to be rather tough on Turkey if this turns out to be necessary; it is significant that German policy has become much more severe. The Lisbon European Council confirmed the plans to offer Turkey an improved variant of association for the time being.

Germany is, on the whole, very favourable to enlargement, since it would strengthen its neighbourly ties with Austria and Switzerland in the southeast and the Nordic countries around the Baltic sea. All the candidate countries have close economic and financial relations with Germany, which is their largest trading partner among the EC countries. Austria and Switzerland have long belonged to the D-mark zone, and Sweden has for two years attempted to pursue a tight monetary policy with fixed exchange rates with a unilateral pegging to the ecu, although in 1992 the policy was under severe strain.

Enlargement was singled out as one of the main objectives of the British presidency for the second half of 1992 and the British fought hard at the Lisbon summit at least to be able to open 'unofficial' negotiations with the EFTA applicants during the presidency. Britain still has economic interest in its former EFTA partners, and hopes that they would both strengthen the commitment to free trade and bring to the Community a higher degree of budgetary discipline. Originally, the British government had wanted the accession negotiations to be opened even before the Treaty on EU was ratified. This was not acceptable to the other member states, but the conclusions of the Lisbon summit enabled the British presidency to start preparations for negotiations. The British government's interest in increasing the intergovernmental cooperation within the Union framework is widely believed to be a primary reason for its attachment to enlargement.

Denmark regards the accession of the Nordic countries as an end to the artificial division of the North. Denmark would no longer be the only representative of the Nordic welfare society in the EC and hopes to find additional support for Danish policies in the Council. The accession of Nordic countries would have a favourable impact on Danish public opinion, but the malaise which came to the surface in the referendum of the Treaty on EU showed that the Danes also fear a diminished role of small countries in an enlarged Union. Denmark's position is, however, somewhat ambiguous; attempts to safeguard the interests of smaller member countries might trigger substantial deepening of the EC and thus prove contrary to embedded Danish interests. It is not clear that the link between enlargement and ratification of the Treaty on EU had any impact on how the Danes cast their votes in the referendum in June 1992. Given the turmoil generated by Denmark over Maastricht, Danish support for enlargement might stiffen resistance elsewhere to the prospect.

The Dutch government shares Denmark's concern for strengthening the middle-sized countries' positions and welcomes free-trade-minded countries in the EC. However, the Dutch, together with the other Benelux countries, would not accept an enlargement if it threatened to water down the structures of the Community, or the role of the institutions or the embryonic CFSP. They outlined in the Benelux Memorandum that: 'through enlargement, the institutional and structural adjustments to be made during the accession negotiations will become both unavoidable and desirable. In such a scenario the accession negotiations could fully or partially coincide with the contemplated revision of the Treaty.'[15] Belgium, because of its explicitly stated fears of a watering down of the Community, is perhaps the member state least in favour of enlargement. Belgians see themselves as guardians of the independence of the EC institutions and the endeavour to make the EC more federal.

The Belgian view is much shared by Luxembourg, which is deeply worried about its position as a small member were the rumoured proposals for institutional changes to be discussed seriously.

Portugal shares the view that an EFTA enlargement is beneficial to the Union, but is wary lest enlargement undermine the position of the smaller member countries. Italian views broadly coincide with those of the Dutch, while generally favouring enlargement on the grounds that the EC should be open to the accession of other European countries. Spain welcomes the outcome of the Lisbon summit on enlargement. The Foreign Minister, Javier Solana, told Spanish parliamentarians that it was false to present Spain as being 'reticent' towards enlargement. On the contrary, Spain favoured enlargement of the EC 'with the same conviction with which it favours deepening' and accepted that the start of accession negotiations was 'the only sensible option for those within the Community and for those who hope to join'.[16] For the southern member states and Ireland, the link between enlargement and the ratification of the Treaty on EU and the completion of the budget negotiations was of vital importance, since their entering into force ensures the vital interest of economic and social cohesion of these countries.

The French believe that the Community has first to consolidate its internal development, as agreed in the Treaty on EU, and that enlargement should never be allowed to destabilize the Community. French officials describe the country's position as prudently positive, but are keen to embed the CFSP at the next IGC conference in 1996, before new members are let in. Consequently, the French stress the need for compliance with the *finalités politiques* of the Treaty on EU and worry whether neutrality is compatible with it. President Mitterrand has on several occasions advocated his own idea of the future shape of Europe. He has, for example, argued for a wider European framework, beyond the Community, in the shape of a Confederation which would include the east Europeans in a larger European circle without undermining the EC itself. Though the proposal did not fly when originally mooted, it may yet re-emerge in the debate.[17] Along the lines of the same idea, President Mitterrand proposed to hold summit meetings of the Heads of State and Government of the Council of Europe. This statement was welcomed by the Turkish Prime Minister, Suleyman Demirel, currently holder of the rotating presidency, who said that this 'would create the perfect opportunity to remodel the Council of Europe's role in an enlarged Europe, its relationship with the CSCE, as well as any new tasks it may be assigned'.[18]

The evolving position of the Commission

The Commission was given the task by the European Council in Maastricht of examining the implications of enlargement. To fulfil this request, it set up an inter-services task force, which presented its report, 'Europe and the Challenge of Enlargement', in June 1992 to the Lisbon meeting (see Appendix 3). The report, added to the Conclusions of the Presidency, found a 'remarkable consensus' among the member states, considering their different starting positions, and made 'a very good contribution' to the discussion which 'helped to reach a consensus'.[19]

The Commission in its nuanced report reconfirms the importance for the applicant countries to accept fully the *acquis*, including the Treaty on EU and the political objectives it enshrines.

In the area of CFSP the report stresses that applicant countries should be left in no doubt that membership of the Union implies the development of a common defence and that 'specific and binding assurances will be sought from them with regard to their political commitment and legal capacity to fulfil the obligations'. The Community, the report argues, is attractive because it is seen to be effective: 'to proceed to enlargement in a way which reduces its effectiveness would be an error'. Therefore, with the prospect of a Union of 20 or 30 members, the question is now to ensure that 'the new Union can function, taking account of the fact that the system for two of its pillars is intergovernmental'.

The question of neutrality and its compatibility with the CFSP is 'a particular concern'. The Commission considers the accession of the EFTA countries which have applied for membership should not pose insuperable problems of an economic nature. The report deals carefully with the applications of Turkey, Cyprus and Malta, suggesting that, though membership is not yet appropriate, these countries' relations with the Community should be pursued and upgraded. For the other European countries which have not yet applied for membership a system of 'new partnership' should be created so as to take into account their need for close economic and political links with the Community. The Commission believes that 'new means should be created for this purpose [i.e. to respect their will to be treated as equal partners], building upon the existing "architecture" of European organizations so as to create a "European political area"'. The Commission concludes in its report that the challenge of enlargement must be met with a strategy 'that is inspired not only by practical consideration of what is possible in the near future, but by a vision of the wider Europe which must be imagined and prepared in the longer term. That is why the Commission proposes a strategy of opening negotiations soon with those countries which are ready and able to join, and preparing the way actively for others who may come later.'

The report confirms that the Commission prefers enlargement in waves to a one-by-one approach, with groups of candidate countries being treated together and parallel negotiations being conducted on issues specific to individual countries. This strategy would make the Community's task more manageable and facilitate the adoption of EC institutions and policies. It also increases the pressures on hesitant EFTA governments to submit applications sooner rather than later.

Technically, the Commission sees relatively few problems in the negotiations with EFTA candidates. They have, after all, already taken on board some 60% of the *acquis communautaire* through the EEA. The most contentious area will be agriculture, where the outcome will be a matter of tough negotiations with the member states. Some candidates – Finland and Switzerland, as well as Norway if it applies – are likely to ask for long transitional periods and some special treatment, and most EFTA countries have extensive and economically inefficient agricultural policies, linked to their regional policies, which will all call for special consideration. Fisheries and alpine transit will certainly be other tricky dossiers.

The report on enlargement and the opinion on Sweden's application for membership underline the Commission's concern that neutral candidate countries might affect negatively the *acquis* of the Union in the area of CFSP. It is the reason why the Commission plans to ask applicants for 'specific and binding assurances' to ensure that their political commitment and legal capacity make them able to accept the *acquis politique*. The Commission is, however, aware that the applicant EFTA countries' various concepts of neutrality are distinct and originate from different historical and political experiences and have different legal foundations. Insights into the characteristics of these concepts are important, if others are to comprehend the redefinitions of neutrality which are under way and to evaluate the applicants' willingness to give the assurances sought. Although there can be no permanent exception for neutrality, the Treaty on EU gives in Article J.4.4 at least to the current neutral member, Ireland, the opportunity to pursue, to a certain degree, its traditional policy.[20] But on balance, the Commission has so far held the pragmatic view that neutrality is mainly a political problem to which a solution could be found during the accession negotiations.

Before the Danish referendum on the Treaty on EU, it seemed that the Commission favoured further institutional reforms, both in general and to underpin enlargement. However, in the wake of the Danish referendum, it has, after some internal debate, endorsed the view that an enlargement of EFTA applicants might take place without institutional changes beyond those triggered by the accession itself. Here they appeared to side with those who argue that, in the short term, adaptations in line with the provisions of the Treaty on EU would suffice as regards numbers of Commissioners per country, the voting procedures and presidency of the Council and the number of members of the European Parliament, though it should be noted that the EC has yet to reach final decisions on the size of the Commission and the Parliament. In any event, the next IGC – already foreseen for 1996 – could address the question of more far-reaching institutional reform. Others have argued the case for bringing forward the IGC, or at least starting to prepare for

it now, addressing basic constitutional and administrative principles. The argument runs that a 'deepening' reform is necessary to
prepare for an EC that would have to accommodate more small
member countries and countries needing a much higher degree of
financial support, while ensuring the effectiveness of the EC's
institutions in enhancing the democratic aspects of EU. The Commission backed away from supporting this position at Lisbon.

The Commission also proposed a different strategy concerning
the central and east European countries. The Europe Agreements
and the Phare programme are seen as important instruments to
provide the political and economic support that would prepare
Hungary, the CSFR and Poland for eventual membership of the
Community. The steps already taken towards building a partnership with the Visegrad countries would be strengthened by even
closer cooperation and consultation at a political level, to be
extended in due course to Bulgaria and Romania. Officials in the
Commission recognize that the economic and political problems in
central and eastern Europe are so great that it will take these
countries quite some time to be ready to assume the requirements
of full membership of the EC. Vice-Commissioner Frans Andriessen
has stressed the importance of the Community to 'foster the sense
of belonging to the wider European family of democratic peoples
by creating new political and economic ties'.[21] There is some
discussion in the Commission as to how far membership of WEU
or of NATO might satisfy some of these needs, as well as whether
a strengthening of the Council of Europe and CSCE would be
useful.

The Commission is also keen to promote regional cooperation
between the central and east European countries through the
Europe Agreements. Some officials in the Commission question
whether the wish of Poland, Hungary and the CSFR to become
members of the EC will fade, once they have realized the extent to
which they would have to qualify their newly regained sovereignty.

As to southern candidate countries, the Commission's views
are similar to those in the EC member states. Preoccupations are

centred primarily upon the institutional implications of the accession of small states (Malta or Cyprus), or the economic, social and political implications of accepting Turkey, a poorer country with a large population and with somewhat different cultural values and political norms. It should be remembered that in 1976 the Commission's report on the Greek application cautioned against Greek accession.[22]

Even though the success and influence of current small member states of the EC are not questioned, many people in the Commission wonder whether Malta or Cyprus would be able to assume full responsibilities in the EC institutions or are ready to manage complicated EC dossiers in their national administrations. The partition of Cyprus is a difficult political problem. The Greek administration of the island has assured the Community of the feasibility of membership, but the Commission remains sceptical for both practical and political reasons, concluding that the two should not be in the 'first wave' of enlargement.

The case of Turkey is accepted as needing special attention. Turkey has been in the pipeline for membership for 30 years and demands with some justified vigour fair treatment from the EC. Nevertheless, the Commission maintains the position outlined in its Opinion of 1989 on a Turkish membership, in which it is stated that membership cannot yet be on the agenda, since the country does not fulfil economic and social conditions for accession.[23] Turkey's poor record in the area of human rights is also held against it.

It was rumoured that the Commission's report on enlargement bore signs of internal disagreement between Frans Andriessen, the Commissioner responsible for external relations, and President Jacques Delors. Jacques Delors wanted, after the Danish referendum on the Treaty on EU, to 'emphasize the EC's new concern not to intrude on the prerogatives of national governments and to suppress any suggestion that the accession of new EC members will automatically trigger a new phase of tighter integration'. Frans Andriessen, it was reported, had stuck to the belief that any enlargement necessitates institutional reform.[24] Whether or not such reports give a true picture of the discussion on enlargement within the Commission, the Commissioners themselves have become more careful to avoid prompting suggestions of the kind that were inappropriately attributed to Jacques Delors in the Danish referendum and which certainly influenced the internal Danish debate. The rumours of plans to reduce the role of small countries fuelled Danish fears that their influence would be curtailed within the European Union.[25]

Delors had been cited as warning the member states about the 'political, intellectual and institutional shock' which would come in the Commission's report on enlargement. His personal reflections on institutional reform were interpreted as an explicit call for radical changes necessitated by enlargement.[26] President Delors clarified his position when he stated after a foreign ministers' meeting in Portugal in May 1992 that 'in a new architecture of Europe profound institutional changes will be needed'. This 'should not take place in the coming two years, but it would be dishonest to believe that deepening and widening go together and do not pose serious contradictions'.[27] At the time of writing, the Commission's approach rested with its published report for Lisbon, a prudent statement that deliberately eschewed radical propositions, even though it was widely recognized that this did not close the debate on what might eventually be required. Some hints of the need to develop the debate remained in the reference to a 'European Political Area' for the larger Europe. Here there were echoes of an earlier comment on the problems of diversity that an enlarged Community would pose, by Vice-President Frans Andriessen when he launched his idea of 'affiliate membership'.[28] Affiliate membership would 'provide membership and obligations in some areas, while excluding others, at least for a transitional period. It would give the affiliate members a seat at the Council table on a par with full members in specified areas, together with appropriate representation in other institutions, such as the Parliament.' Criticism of Andriessen's concept was heard both from within the Commission itself and from the member states. The concept has so far not been extended or worked out in more detail.

The debate in the European Parliament

The European Parliament has in principle welcomed enlargement of the Community on the condition that the accession of new members should not endanger its fundamental principles and structures. This view was expressed in a report from the Political Affairs Committee in March 1991.[29] The Committee considered that the EC 'should as soon as possible initiate negotiations with European countries wishing to join the Community provided they meet the necessary political and economic requirements and are willing to contribute actively to the implementation of the aims of Political Union'. The Committee also pointed out that in the forthcoming negotiations it should be underlined that 'the political, economic and security aspects of European cooperation are closely linked and cannot be artificially separated without jeopardizing the aims of Political Union'. The Foreign Affairs and Security Committee is currently working on a further report taking into account the most recent developments.

In the resolution on the results of the IGCs passed in April 1992, the European Parliament stressed 'that it will not be able to agree to the accession of new Member States unless further reforms are adopted in addition to the Maastricht Treaty, in particular concerning the elimination of the democratic deficit and the consolidation of the principles and aims on which Political Union is based'.[30] The European Parliament has a *de facto* veto-power through the procedure of co-decision, which provides for its assent before enlargement can take place. MEPs have repeated the significance of the resolution on several occasions in the hope that it will be borne in mind by the member states and the applicant countries. Egon Klepsch, President of the European Parliament, underlined in his speech to the European Council in Lisbon that, however positive it is towards an EFTA enlargement, its position on the timing of the next IGC differs from the views of the Commission and the member states: 'I believe that it is essential to convene a conference on institutional reform in parallel with the accession negotiations. I find it unrealistic to postpone this issue to the 1996 review conference provided for in the Maastricht Treaty.'[31]

The parliamentarians have also debated a report on institutional changes (the Hänsch Report), which would be brought about by an enlargement of the Community. This report has caused concern in smaller member states, since it advocates a new institutional model in which the presidency of the Council should change every year according to a system of rotation involving only Germany, Spain, France, Italy and the UK; the other member states should appoint two Vice-Presidents, and all decisions should be taken by majority voting.[32]

Individual MEPs have expressed their opinions on enlargement. Many are concerned over the institutional structure of the EC, pointing out that 'enlargement would be impossible unless the European Parliament first becomes a true co-legislator'.[33] Others have discussed the practical implications if the European Parliament were to embrace more members.[34] An EFTA enlargement would bring the number of MEPs to 656, and were the CSFR, Hungary and Poland to become members, this would imply 767 MEPs, according to the principle of 'degressive proportionality' (the higher the population of a country, the lower the ratio of MEPs to the population as a whole). The European Parliament's new building in Brussels will be able to house 750 MEPs in plenary sessions. Enlargement might also put a stop to the constant moves between Brussels, Strasbourg and Luxembourg, which many MEPs consider impossible if their numbers were to increase. There are ideas about finding ways of associating the framework of the Council of Europe and its Assembly with parliamentary debates in the European Parliament on issues that concern the whole of Europe. This would be a means of creating a forum for discussion between the Community and European countries outside the EC without endangering the structure of the former. Most MEPs have argued for a necessary linkage between enlargement and the Delors-2 package, underlining the principle of financial solidarity among the members of the Community.

2.3 The process of ratification of the Treaty on European Union
Enlargement was linked to the entry into force of the Treaty on EU
by the statement of the European Council in Lisbon in June 1992.
The difficulties over ratification have been clear both in those
countries which have held referenda and in the UK, where the
parliamentary procedure has also provoked deep controversy. The
referenda in Denmark, Ireland and France have revealed a gap
between national politicians and their constituents, and an even
wider gap between the institutions in Brussels and the population
in the member states. But the referenda have also become trapped
in national politics, where the popularity of the established parties
and of governments has been tested. The malaise towards the
treaty first emerged in Denmark, but has since then influenced
doubters and opponents to the Union elsewhere, in both current
member states and applicant countries. With the ratification process still incomplete, several implications for enlargement emerge:

* the timetable for the opening of negotiations with EFTA
  applicants is likely to be delayed;
* doubts persist about what the *acquis* of the Union would
  comprise if special status clauses were granted to current
  members;
* the debate for and against a two-speed Union has a bearing
  on the positions of member states, as regards both the timing
  of the negotiations and the next IGC, which could become
  limited to the arrangements for accession; and
* public opinion in the applicant countries could be influenced
  by the deep-rooted hesitancy towards the Union felt by some
  citizens of the current EC member states.

The Danish referendum
The Danish population rejected the Treaty on EU in a referendum
of 2 June 1992 (an event that some liken to the French National
Assembly's rejection of the Treaty on European Defence Community in 1954), albeit by a narrow margin – 50.7% of the population
voted against and 49.3% in favour. Although some polls predicted

this, the first reaction was one of total surprise, both in Denmark and in other member states. The referendum on the Treaty on EU went in the opposite direction to the one on the Single European Act in 1986, when the Danish parliament had voted against ratification, but the SEA had been 'saved' by the positive result in the referendum. In May 1992, the Danish parliament voted in favour of the Treaty on EU by a overwhelming majority (130 to 25), but this could not overturn the verdict of the people. Many commentators interpreted the referendum result as a vote of no-confidence not only in the EU, but also in Danish politicians, who had become too distant from the people.

The Treaty on EU stipulates in Article R that the entry into force occurs after ratification by the High Contracting parties. No provision was made for non-ratification by one or more EC members, partly because this would have had an adverse psychological effect; there was therefore no contingency plan for the result of the Danish referendum. The Portuguese presidency issued a statement, after an emergency meeting of the EC foreign ministers in Oslo, saying that there was 'strong unanimity that the Eleven should go ahead, without any hesitation, to fulfil the [Maastricht] obligations'. The foreign ministers underlined that there was 'no room for renegotiating' the treaty.[35] The EC presidency statement was buttressed by a joint statement from President Mitterrand and Chancellor Kohl, in which 'France and Germany jointly assert their determination firmly and coherently to pursue the implementation of the European Union ... The door to European Union will remain open to Denmark'.[36] Also the British Prime Minister, John Major, defended the ratification of the treaty in a debate in the House of Commons on 4 June, arguing that 'the ratification and implementation of the treaty is in our national interest, and we shall continue during our presidency to work for the Community we secured in that negotiation'.[37] At the time, the Danish Foreign Minister, Uffe Elleman-Jensen, did not ask for a renegotiation of the treaty 'because it would be impossible', but stressed that what was now needed was a 'long time for reflection'.[38]

The political leaders of the Community adopted a policy of

'business as usual' after the Danish referendum, pressing on with their national ratification processes and leaving the Danes (at their own request) to find the best possible solution to the problem. But, in the aftermath of the vote, it became clear that the Danish rejection had had a huge impact on the further ratification of the treaty and on the Community as a whole. First came the decision of the French President, François Mitterrand, to opt for a referendum on the treaty instead of ratification by a parliamentary process. Second, a more hostile climate emerged in the national debates over the treaty, notably in the UK, where Tory backbenchers who disagreed with the government's line on European integration became more vocal. Third, the changing responses from the Commission, especially President Delors himself, initially stressed the relevance of the principle of subsidiarity as a means of reassuring opinion in the member states about the limits to Community powers.

Legal experts have analysed the legal consequences of the Danish rejection of the treaty and have referred to the Vienna Convention on Treaties. This provides for treaties to be revised by common agreement by all parties concerned, with the possibility that the revisions might apply to only some signatories. The legal experts of the ECU Institute in Lyon, for example, concluded that the general democratic principle of the Community might be held to prevent a very small majority of Community citizens from blocking the progress of the Community. As the 'defaulting state put itself on the fringe of the Community', the others could remain disposed to 'allow the state to rejoin the Community'. Legally, 'a technical complement to the Maastricht Treaty is thus necessary', which could take the form of a complementary protocol, which would have to be approved by all member states including Denmark.[39]

The reasons behind the Danish people's rejection of the Treaty on EU are as many as they are varied. The Danish position on European integration, in parliament and among the public, has always stressed economic integration and been more ambivalent about political integration. The word 'union' has the same connotation for the Danes as the word 'federation' has for the British; it evokes experiences from the past, such as the Kalmar Union, or the Union with Norway. In the run-up to the referendum on the Single European Act in 1986, Prime Minister Schlüter had assured the Danish voters that 'the Union is dead'. The word 'Union', which appears in the preamble to the Act, was never before translated literally into Danish. Some say *'sammenslutning'* – a binding together – might have been more acceptable.

Several other issues caused concern in Denmark, in particular a possible common defence policy and the final stage of the EMU, in both cases linked to fears of German dominance (even though the Danish krone has long been pegged to the D-mark). The prospects of Nordic enlargement did not offset these fears, not least because the increased number of small states might provoke proposals to diminish the role of all small states, as well as complicate certain policy areas, such as the CAP. Danish worries were also evident about the EC impact on the social welfare system, inflows of immigrants and lower environmental standards.

Polls taken during the summer of 1992 revealed increasing opposition to EU. In August, for instance, 57% of the voters would have rejected the treaty.[40] On the other hand, a poll in September suggested that 64% of the Danes would accept European Union were Denmark to obtain exemptions to certain areas in the treaty. This poll showed continuing opposition to a single currency, a European central bank and a Community asylum policy, but some lessening of opposition to a common defence policy and a common foreign policy.[41]

Prime Minister Schlüter announced, after a meeting with the leaders of parties represented in parliament, the framework within which Denmark's position vis-à-vis the Treaty on EU might evolve. The government's aim is to find a way for Denmark to continue to participate in the EC. A White Paper, published on 12 October, outlines various alternatives. A new referendum could be organized during spring or early autumn 1993, but it must be held on a new political basis, and the government expects the Danish case to be negotiated at the Edinburgh European Council in December or at a special IGC. Prime Minister Schlüter has stressed the importance of the principle of subsidiarity and of limiting the competences of the Commission.[42] He has on several occasions ruled out the possibility of a two-speed Europe.

The Irish referendum

On 18 June 1992, two weeks after the Danish rejection, the Irish population endorsed the Treaty on EU with a comfortable two-thirds majority. As in the previous SEA referendum, many opponents concentrated their arguments on the provisions on common defence, but the most heated debate was on the question of abortion. Groups both for and against abortion, which is illegal in Ireland according to the constitution, argued against the treaty. Ireland had inserted a protocol in the Treaty on EU that stated its compatibility with these provisions of the Irish constitution. The issue came to the fore when a 14-year-old rape victim was refused the right to leave Ireland to have an abortion. Her lawyers claimed that this infringed the right of free movement of people within the EC. The Irish Supreme Court ruled that the girl could have an abortion even in Ireland on health grounds, leaving the free movement issue unresolved. Doubts as to the implications of the protocol persist. None the less, a very strong case was made for the fundamental importance of EC membership for the Irish economy – Ireland receives substantial financial support from EC funds and would be a major beneficiary of the proposed new cohesion fund. This argument proved persuasive.

The French referendum

In the wake of the negative result in the Danish referendum, President Mitterrand decided to call for a referendum in France on 20 September 1992. The decision was interpreted as a means for him to recover popularity for his presidency. The alternative route of ratifying the treaty in parliament would have been less risky. President Mitterrand, however, wanted a public endorsement of his policy on Europe, as well as to damage the right-wing opposition, already strongly divided over Maastricht. The National Assembly and the Senate, meeting together in the Congress of

71

Versailles on 23 June 1992, adopted by a large majority (592 to 73) the amendments necessary to the French constitution to ratify the Treaty on EU.

The referendum campaign opened in July 1992, with opinion polls showing a comfortable majority in favour. A poll in June had indicated 62% in favour and 38% against, with approximately a third likely to abstain. But by August opinion polls showed declining support for Maastricht, with 57% in favour and 45% against.[43] This trend continued until the end of August, when opinion polls indicated a slight majority against. The government and the supporters of Maastricht had to redouble their efforts to convince the French to vote in favour. President Mitterrand's intervention in a three-hour television appearance on 3 September seems to have stopped the gains of the anti-Maastricht campaign, and opinion polls showed support back at 55%.

Supporters of the Treaty on EU included the governing Socialist Party, which was solidly in favour (only Jean-Pierre Chevènement resigned from the party's executive bureau on the issue), and Socialist voters largely followed the leadership. The UDF, traditionally a pro-European party under the leadership of Valéry Giscard d'Estaing, broadly supported Maastricht, though Philippe de Villiers, also from the UDF, joined the campaign against the treaty. The leadership of the two Green parties, Génération Ecologique and les Verts, were in favour, though their electorates and MPs remained divided.

The treaty's opponents comprised an unprecedented combination of extreme right and left, as well as the Gaullist RPR. The RPR leader, Jacques Chirac, pronounced himself feebly in favour, in an attempt to avoid a split in the party, but two firm opponents of the treaty, Charles Pasqua and Philippe Séguin, campaigned forcefully for a 'no', and carried much of the RPR electorate with them. The Communist Party and the right-wing Front National were strongly against the treaty, as well as any move towards closer European integration, and were largely supported by their voters.[44]

The referendum campaign also threw into question President

Mitterrand's future. Many anti-Maastricht campaigners argued for the President's resignation in the event of a rejection of the treaty. Although the President himself repeated endlessly that this was not the issue, the 'stake Mitterrand'[45] became increasingly mixed up with the future of the Union.

Some provisions in the treaty particularly worried the French electorate, notably the right for all EC citizens to vote and to stand in local elections. This provision became entangled with fears of immigration and the erosion of French national identity. In France, more than many other EC member states, local politicians play a very important role, both in local administration and in electing senators. The amendments to the French constitution to implement Maastricht, however, deny EC citizens the right to become mayor or vice-mayor or to participate in the election of senators. The EMU was seen by the opponents of the Union as giving up essential French sovereignty over economic and monetary matters. On the other hand, its supporters tried to ride on fears of German dominance, arguing that the only way to strengthen the ties between France and Germany was to implement a real EMU and Political Union. A strong current of antipathy to Germany permeated the referendum campaign generally, and was used by both sides to reinforce their arguments.

The outcome of the referendum was a narrow vote in favour (51.01%). This victory, however narrow, greatly relieved political leaders in Europe, who hoped it would calm unstable money markets. President Mitterrand, however, declared that there were no winners or losers, acknowledging the feeling of those citizens who by voting 'no' had wanted to safeguard strongly held values. Jacques Delors, who had put his future in office at stake, declared that the positive vote was decisive progress for the Community. He confirmed that the anxiety of the 'no' voters would be taken into account at both the national and the European level, for which a deepening of democratic practices was essential.[46]

The supporters of the treaty could largely be found in the richer constituencies, less touched by unemployment, and in areas where the rate of immigrants is lower. City dwellers and those in boarder regions were more favourable – in Strasbourg (72.2%), Rennes (69.9%) and Paris (62.51%), while much of the agricultural population was against. The supporters were strikingly composed of young and retired people, as well as those with a high income and good education. This presents President Mitterrand with a paradox, since he had secured the victory in the presidential election with the support of a different electorate.[47] If the general election of March 1993 were to produce a majority for the right and there were a new period of cohabitation, a new government would face a difficult task in agreeing on a joint European policy.

Luxembourg
Luxembourg ratified the Treaty on EU on 2 July 1992, with a vote in the Chamber of Deputies of 51 votes to 6. The Chamber also amended the Luxembourg constitution with provisions on EMU and on the right of vote and to stand in a local election for EC citizens. On the latter point a compromise was reached by which only those EC citizens who have lived in Luxembourg for ten years and who speak Luxembourg languages will be eligible to stand as town councillors, but they will not have the right to stand as mayor or aldermen. The compromise was necessitated by the level of EC citizens (28.5%) in the total population of 400,000 people.[48]

Greece
The Greek parliament adopted the treaty on 1 August with an overwhelming majority of 286 to 8. All the main parliamentary parties supported the treaty, with only some Communist representatives voting against. The vote in the parliament was brought forward several months in order to avoid the treaty becoming embroiled with the issue of membership in WEU, which will be settled in late 1992. Given the history of Greek domestic debate on Europe, this overwhelming support for Maastricht was particularly striking.

Other member states
All other member states, with the exception of the UK, have kept their timetables on the process of ratification, and are aiming to conclude it by the end of the year.

Belgium: the House of Representatives voted in favour of the bill (146 to 33), approving the treaty in July. The ratification process was subsequently resumed in the Senate.

Germany: there was a difficult debate over the likely impact of EU on the division of powers between the Länder and the federal government. Agreement was reached between representatives of the Bundestag and the Länder that an amendment to Article 23 of the constitution was needed in order to give the Bundesrat the right to approve any transfer of sovereignty to the Union and to give the Länder a right to review decisions taken in the context of the Union in areas which fall under the exclusive competence of the Länder, namely education and the police. The government might depute Länder officials to represent Germany in the relevant Community bodies. In other areas the Länder will have the right to influence the definition of the government's policy, which should take their opinions into account.[49] The Bundesrat opened the debate on the treaty on 25 September, and the Bundestag opened its debate on October 8. It was also evident that EMU and the 'abandonment' of the D-mark created serious concern and controversy in Germany, so much so that a hypothetical referendum could have produced an overwhelming popular rejection of Maastricht. The sensitivity of the issue is such that the German government would have to go back for parliamentary endorsement of any move to the third stage of EMU.

Italy: the Senate approved the treaty in September, and full ratification is expected by the end of the year.

The Netherlands: the treaty is expected to be ratified by parliament by the end of the year.

Portugal: parliament is expected to ratify the treaty during the autumn.

Spain: the Spanish Congress of Representatives approved in July the draft reform of the constitution that was needed to make it conform to the treaty. The Congress of Representatives resumed the debate on the treaty on 1 October, with a view to concluding by the end of the year. However, the intense importance which the Spanish attach to the cohesion issue should mean that final ratification of Maastricht will be pegged to EC-wide agreement on the Delors-2 package. It is not that Spanish commitment to Maastricht is in doubt, but that their concern is to maximize leverage on the budgetary negotiations, a concern that can only have been accentuated by the problems of the peseta in the wake of the September currency crises.

The United Kingdom: the Danish referendum result had a profound impact on the debate in the UK over Maastricht and on the timetable for parliamentary ratification. It had been the government's intention to bring the bill back to parliament before the summer recess, but this was postponed *sine die* in June, once it became clear just how extensive and vocal opposition was on the Conservative Party's own backbenches. In particular, politicians and political commentators were taken aback to find criticism not only from the older 'Thatcherite' generation, but also from the new intake of younger MPs – 'Thatcher's children'. Over the summer, the government equivocated, helped by the silence of the Labour Party, which was in the throes of electing a new leader, and the pending French referendum. Ministers agreed prudently on the need to see how Danish thinking evolved, although these events hardly provided an auspicious start to the UK presidency of the Council.

At the beginning of September 1992, John Major had apparently calmly stated that the British government would await the outcome of *both* French and Danish deliberations before proceeding to ratification in the UK. In a speech in September 1992, John Major stated:

> the individual nations, through their democratic procedures, must have the final say. And that is why if Denmark, and France, or any other member states, says 'No', than all must think again. There can be no question of leaving one member behind. Britain would not be a party to such an agreement...[50]

76

This calm was to be shattered by the extraordinary events which led to Britain's unilateral retreat from the ERM and *de facto* devaluation of sterling. These events simultaneously threw into question *both* the government's economic policy *and* its European policy, as opponents of Maastricht seized on the moment to indicate their long-argued case against EMU and were joined by critics of the incompetence of the government. The extent of this crisis cannot be underestimated – analogies abound, the worst crisis since Suez or at least since de Gaulle's rejection of British accession to the EC in 1963.

For several days a beleaguered and apparently divided government made no clear declarations of intent, although much blame was heaped on the Bundesbank for having allegedly encouraged speculation against sterling. In the end, after a tense discussion in cabinet, it was announced on 1 October 1992 that the government intended to hold to its intention to ratify Maastricht and to bring the bill back to parliament in December or early in the new year. John Major in this sense tied his own future to Maastricht in spite of having failed to retain what had been a firm commitment to the ERM. Tense debate followed at an unprecedentedly rowdy Conservative Party Conference in October. The government's position was further weakened by the crisis over the coal industry. This found backbench conservatives surprisingly vocal in their criticisms of government policy and even more determined to resist the ratification of Maastricht.

Meanwhile the Labour Party, under its new leader John Smith, was faced with a difficult challenge in formulating a Labour position on Maastricht. There were important opponents of Maastricht within the party, in particular Brian Gould, the defeated leadership candidate. It was tempting to exploit the government's severe weaknesses, especially on the version of Maastricht which included the opt-out on the social chapter. However, the new leadership took an apparently very firm position in favour of Maastricht and against a referendum. With Brian Gould's resignation from the shadow cabinet and the relative weakness of his supporters on this issue, it looks at the time of writing as if the

Labour Party's position is now rather well-defined. However, the continuing problems of the government on so many fronts make all predictions dangerous.

This saga has left the UK presidency of the Council in severe straits. An extraordinarily convened European Council in Birmingham on 16 October was momentarily seen as an opportunity to deal with the 'fault-lines' of the ERM and a radical declaration on subsidiarity to get both Danes and British off the hook. But neither was forthcoming. Thus decisions were deferred to the Edinburgh European Council, if not beyond. As regards enlargement, even though German and French statements had continued to acknowledge its continuing necessity, it had become virtually impossible for the British presidency to occupy the high ground in advocating speedy enlargement. British difficulties had also re-opened a debate on a 'two-speed' Europe, at least behind the scenes – a scenario which would necessarily have profound implications for an enlarged Community.

3

Potential new EC members

3.1 The EFTA states

Austria

Austria was the first EFTA country to hand in its membership application to the EC. The decision, taken in 1989, came after two years of intensive debate on how to shape the country's future relations with the Community. Since then, Austria has taken part in the negotiations between the EC and EFTA to set up the EEA, but has never doubted that it was only membership which could give it full access to rights and obligations of the Community.

This recent debate on membership started in 1987 and was triggered by the increasingly dynamic developments in the Community which clearly necessitated a revision of Austrian policy towards the EC.[1] The Foreign Minister, Alois Mock, coined a new concept, the 'global approach', which would ensure Austria's full participation in the internal market while leaving aside the precise institutional framework. When referring to this concept, the Austrian government did not exclude the possibility of full membership. It had commissioned a special report whose conclusions, presented in 1988, were that only EC membership would grant real sovereignty (as opposed to formal sovereignty), in a world where states were becoming increasingly interdependent. Although Austria continued its efforts to find a way to gain access to the internal market, the Community made it clear that only members of the EC could participate on an equal footing in the decision-making process, and that the internal structures could not be loosened in order to make room for a non-member country.

Since the EC had made clear to Austria that half-way alternatives to membership were not acceptable, President Delors's speech in January 1989 came as a surprise to many Austrians. His offer to create a new, more structured, relationship between the EC and the EFTA countries was widely interpreted as a way to ward off the Austrian membership application. Already from the outset of the EEA process, Austrian politicians were somewhat sceptical about what the negotiations could offer in terms of real influence in the EC decision-making process, and were not ready to change Austria's policy towards that of the EC from what had been staked out. At the same time, the EEA process was regarded as a good opportunity to prepare the country for adaptations necessary for EC membership by incorporating a large part of the *acquis communautaire* into Austrian legislation. Finally, as a member of EFTA, Austria was included in the process towards closer integration with the EC.

In July 1989, Austria tabled its EC membership application. The application enjoyed strong support from the ruling 'grand coalition' composed of the two major parties, the Austrian People's Party and the Social Democrats, the parliament and the social partners. The important organizations of the social partners, employers, farmers and labour, all supported the government's initiative. In order to ensure a wholehearted endorsement of the application, the government chose to insert a paragraph on Austria's neutrality. But there is consensus that the clause reflects the political situation of Europe before the fall of the Berlin Wall; so, if the application had been handed in under the political circumstances of 1992, the clause would most certainly not have been included. Austrian politicians assume that a way will be found during the accession negotiations to accommodate Austria's neutrality status in the Community framework and stress that in future solidarity with its European partners will take precedence over neutrality.

Important reasons for the Austrian decision to seek membership of the EC are to be found in the economic area; the industrial lobby has been one of the strongest forces behind the application. Austria's industry relies heavily on exports (65%) to and imports (68%) from the Community.[2] Integration has been seen as an instrument of structural policy which would aim at a thorough process of liberalization and opening-up in the socio-economic field.[3] The Austrian economy is based on small and middle-sized companies, which to a large extent operate domestically. The low degree of internationalization makes Austrian companies even more dependent on exports than counterparts in several other EFTA partners. One striking feature of the Austrian economy is the large public sector dating back to the post-war period. Integration with the internal market of the EC would boost competition and result in lower prices on goods and services, access to research-and-development programmes to promote modernization and technical innovation, and a general increase of the GNP per year in the region of 3.5%.

The government claims that the agricultural sector would benefit from being able to compete with products from the EC member countries on equal terms.[4] This argument, however, is not shared by the farmers. They form one of the groups least in favour of EC membership, since the CAP is less generous in financial support than Austrian agricultural policy. The farmers have traditionally voted for the Austrian People's Party, which was the first convinced pro-European party (now joined by the Social Democrats, who are firmly in favour of accession to the EC). Although the economic advantages to be expected from membership are considerable, Austria's motives for wishing to join the EC are heavily based on political considerations. Austria is conscious that the EC has come to be a vital element in European affairs, whose decisions have consequences for all European countries.

Events in eastern Europe and the break-up of the Soviet Union have had a positive impact, by making irrelevant Soviet attitudes to Austrian membership of the EC. The Austrians have long argued for active Community involvement in restructuring new market economies, stabilizing fragile democracies and creating a new security structure for Europe. Austria also criticized the EC for responding inadequately to the Yugoslav crises, and has in the past expressed some concern that the community might not fully assist Hungary, the CSFR and Poland in building up their economies by granting free access to EC markets.[5] Given their geography and history, it is natural that Austrians should take a keen interest in these matters. In the early stages of the revolutions in eastern Europe, there was an anti-EC tendency in Austria, which rested its case on building up *Mitteleuropa* rather than pursuing EC membership. This has now more or less faded away, largely because *Mitteleuropa* could never become a substitute for EC membership. In addition, the central and east European countries have all taken the Community as their point of reference. The Green Party is also opposed to the EC, though it has lately begun to modify its position. Its arguments are focused primarily on ecological issues, the agreement between Austria and the EC on road transport being its main target, but it also uses emotional symbols in the debate, such as neutrality or European 'neo-colonialism'.[6]

Austrian neutrality will be a continuing issue, both in the negotiations with the Community and in the internal debate in the run-up to a referendum on EC membership. Neutrality is based on provisions in a federal constitutional law, where Austria declares its permanent neutrality (art. 1), and will not join any military alliances or permit the establishment of any foreign military bases on its territory (art. 2). The status of permanent neutrality became binding under international law through a notification process. The implications for Austrian membership of the EC have been the subject of many conflicting interpretations. But Austria alone is qualified to interpret its neutrality concept in the context of international law and to shape this policy.

Originally, most experts on international law considered Austria's neutrality incompatible with EC membership. This view was still dominant when it handed in its membership application, which accordingly contained a reservation that a future membership should take into account the responsibilities that flow from Austria's status of permanent neutrality. The Austrian government declared that its status of neutrality did not diminish its full acceptance of the ultimate goal of European Union and that it was compatible with the requirements of EC membership.[7] In the Commission's Opinion on Austria's application, it is stated that the negotiations should be based on the *acquis communautaire* as it results from the IGCs. The Commission assessed the economic consequences of Austria's membership in very positive terms, but admitted that permanent neutrality posed problems for the EC as well as for Austria, even before the Treaty on EU was taken into account.[8] The Austrians regard both the application and the Commission's Opinion as somewhat out-of-date concerning neutrality. The Opinion on Sweden's membership application, produced more recently, leads Austrian politicians to expect that the 'specific and binding assurances' the Commission envisages from Sweden in the area of CFSP will also apply to Austria.

The Austrian Foreign Minister made a statement after the signing of the Treaty on EU that 'Austria welcomes the decision on the Economic and Monetary Union ... Austria also attaches particular importance to the Treaty provisions concerning the common foreign and security policy ... [it] will be able as a member state of the Community to make an important contribution to its all-European role ... [and] therefore participate in the common foreign and security policy of the Community actively and in a spirit of solidarity'.[9] The President, Thomas Klestil, reconfirmed Austria's determination to join the EC and thus to take full part in EMU and political union as well as a future European national security system. He stated that 'neutrality is not an end in itself, but serves to defend national security: Austria will therefore pragmatically examine ways of best defending its security, and should be able to take part in a security system based on solidarity, and in which each will protect the other against threats to peace and fundamental rights'.[10]

The Austrian commitment to the Treaty on EU was again underlined in an aide-mémoire submitted to the Community a few weeks before the European Council in Lisbon. The aide-mémoire points out that Austria already fulfilled the conditions for the third stage of the EMU; that, as a future net contributor to the Community budget, it would strengthen economic and social cohesion; that it would contribute politically to the Community through its traditional ties with the countries of central and eastern Europe; that it committed itself fully to the objectives of the European Union and to the further development of security structures, as provided for in the Union treaty with a view to achieving a common foreign and security policy; and, finally, that the institutional implications of an enlargement of the Community should be solved through a step-by-step approach.

The Austrian position is to accept fully the *acquis communautaire* and *politique* of the Treaty on EU as a basis for accession negotiations. Austrian policy-makers have been very concerned to meet the requirements of the *acquis politique* against the background of some considerable domestic reluctance to consider a redefinition of the neutrality concept. Traditionally, neutrality symbolized a mix of economic affluence and national identity built up since the Second World War. Public opinion had associated the neutrality concept with the experience of Switzerland during two world wars, when neutrality proved to be an efficient means of keeping the country away from direct confrontation. The importance of neutrality had become so great that it

> turned into a myth in the eyes of many Austrians; for too long it has been treated as a taboo and, moreover, as a guarantee for Austria's post-war identity. Neutrality, it seems, provided the Austrians with essential means to assert themselves psychologically against German influence.[11]

This resistance to change has been tackled slightly differently by leading politicians. The Foreign Minister has tried to play down the legal implication of neutrality in order to stress the importance of international solidarity and the changes in the political climate of Europe. Austria wanted to show itself a reliable partner in the Gulf war, and also stressed the requirements of solidarity during the Yugoslav crisis. But the Chancellor, Franz Vranitzky of the Social Democratic Party, whose voters are more sensitive on this question, has been more reluctant explicitly to redefine Austrian neutrality.

In the run-up to the referendum on EC membership, the Austrian population's main preoccupations concern not only neutrality but also agriculture, environment, social standards, possible increased transit traffic, and fears of 'Brussels centralism'. Their vote on membership will depend on the outcome of the negotiations with the EC and the extent to which a European security system is being created. According to an Austrian government official, the population is now increasingly aware that European countries are locked in a system of economic, political and social interdependence. Therefore the attempt to stress the importance of European solidarity as the most important element of Austrian security policy seems to be effectively reducing the percentage of the population who regard neutrality as a sticking point.

Public opinion polls on attitudes towards EC membership in summer 1991 showed a lead of 55% to 42% in favour of the EC.[12] In early 1992, however, polls showed that the share of negative votes had increased, reaching nearly 50%. The government has launched an information campaign to try to persuade the public to support EC membership, which seems to have been fairly successful. A September poll showed that 51% of Austrians would have voted in favour of EC membership, while 35% were against and 16% undecided.[13]

Finland[14]

Since November 1991, Finland has moved fast towards EC membership. As late as June 1991, the Finnish Prime Minister, Esko Aho, stated that it was not likely that Finland would become a member of the EC.[15] Seven months later, in February 1992, the Finnish government agreed to put a proposal to the parliament in which it advocated presenting a Finnish application for membership. The parliament's decision to endorse the government's proposal was reached in March 1992, which makes Finland the third EFTA country in the queue to join the Community.

Finland's position in the international context was for a long time strongly influenced by its proximity to the former Soviet Union. The political debate had to find a balance between industry's need for access to EC markets and Soviet suspicion towards too close Finnish links with the EC.[16] Finnish policy-makers chose to approach EFTA and the EC prudently, while reassuring the Soviet government at the same time that closer trade relations with the West would benefit both countries. Finland signed an association agreement with EFTA in 1961. In practical terms this was much the same as full membership, but allowed the government to stress the economic character of cooperation. Only in 1986 did Finland become a full member of EFTA.

At the time of the first EC enlargement, the EFTA countries and Finland signed bilateral free trade agreements with the EEC. The crucial economic links were forged and Finnish industry was able to improve its competitive position in the west European free trade system. Finland has also benefited from close commercial relations with the former USSR. Until the late 1980s, the Soviet share constituted approximately 20% of Finnish foreign trade and was based on imports of raw materials and fuel and exports of manufactured goods. During the oil crises of the 1970s Finland benefited from Soviet oil imports at market prices fixed through a clearing system. Although Finnish industry benefited from export to the Soviet Union, it also protected some sectors of the Finnish economy (for example shipbuilding) from international competition.

During the 1980s, Finnish readiness to integrate more closely with western Europe increased steadily, as a result both of the change in climate between the USSR and the US and of the instability within the Soviet Union caused by radical internal economic and political changes. The Soviet Union was no longer hostile to closer cooperation between Finland and the EC. The new dynamics in the EC, turned into substance by the internal market programme, raised the attractiveness of European markets to Finnish industry, which was especially valuable at a time when Soviet trade had become precarious. Finland therefore welcomed the opening of negotiations between the EC and EFTA in 1989. The

EEA was seen as a route to economic integration with the EC, without raising the difficult issue of membership.

Developments in Finland have gathered pace since summer 1990. There are several reasons for this. The economic climate has worsened considerably as a result of the plunge in Soviet trade (from a 20% to a 5% share of total exports in 1991) that followed the break-up of the Soviet Union. In 1990, the economy suffered its deepest recession of the post-war period. Finnish GNP dropped by 6%; unemployment rates soared to 13%; and financial speculation on the markka increased. Although it was pegged to the ecu in the summer of 1991, the government was forced to devalue in late 1991. The economic difficulties have continued into the second half of 1992, leading to considerable strain within the ruling right-wing coalition and criticism from the Social Democratic opposition. On 8 September 1992, the government decided jointly with Bank of Finland temporarily to abandon its self-imposed peg to the ecu and let the markka float freely – a move which resulted in an immediate drop of 15% in value. The Bank of Finland justified the decision by the disturbances in international currency markets, but maintained that the main task of Finnish monetary policy is to attain monetary stability. It underlined that 'Finnish participation in European integration requires that Finland restores fixed exchange rates with other European currencies when the situation so permits'.[17] During September–October, the government adopted a budget with far-reaching austerity measures to reduce the budget deficit through savings and cost-cutting.

The decision to float the markka was 'deplored' by the European Commission, although the Finnish Under-Secretary of State, Veli Sundbäck, argued that the situation of the markka need not have repercussions as regards the opening of accession negotiations with the Community.[18] On the other hand, there seems to be uneasiness in the Commission about the state and the structure of the Finnish economy, to the effect that Finland's status as a net contributing country might not be clear if the economy does not show signs of recovery.[19]

The political consequences of the collapse of the Soviet Union have given Finland a new freedom of action, but also give rise to uncertainties about Europe's security. Opinion in Finland is divided between those who interpret the new situation to be positive, providing the opportunities to redefine Finnish neutrality, and those who consider it even more dangerous and therefore requiring the classical neutrality concept to be kept intact. Finland has tried, together with the other Nordic countries, to support the efforts of the Baltic states to achieve economic progress and a stable democratic system. This was spelled out in the meeting of the Nordic Council of Ministers in Rönne on the Danish island of Bornholm, when the prime ministers adopted a report which calls for Russian troop withdrawal from the Baltic area. The prime ministers also agreed to cooperate more closely in the foreign and external policy area, in order to present more synchronized views on issues within the EEA and, perhaps later, also in the EC.[20]

The Finnish coalition government's official strategy had been to wait until the EEA negotiations were concluded and then to take a decision on membership. But, in November 1991, when the EEA treaty was heavily delayed by criticisms from the European Court of Justice, Finnish industrialists ran out of patience and subsequently put strong pressure on the government to take action. The outcome of the EEA negotiations has been viewed as unsatisfactory because it conveys little real influence on the decision-making process. But the most decisive factor was the Swedish application for EC membership, which created a feeling of urgency to join, so that negotiations can be conducted in parallel with Sweden and Austria in the first wave of enlargement. Also relevant are the close economic and historical links between Finland and Sweden, which would be disturbed if Sweden alone became a member of the EC. The Finnish President, Mauno Koivisto, who is constitutionally responsible for foreign policy, came out in favour of a Finnish application to the EC in his speech to parliament in February 1992. He had come to the conclusion that because of industry's dependency on foreign markets and the uncertain outcome of the EEA, Finland's interests would be best pursued in the Community context.

The positions of the two main coalition parties on the membership question are conditioned by different preoccupations. The Conservative Party, together with the biggest opposition party, the Social Democratic Party, is in favour of the EC, and the Centre Party, the Prime Minister's party, is divided. Prime Minister Aho campaigned extensively during the first part of 1992 in the north and east of Finland to gain popular support for the government's line. Certain segments of the Centre Party's supporters are strongly against EC membership. They are mainly farmers and people living in sparsely populated areas. The fears of these groups were accommodated in the government's proposition to the parliament, which drew special attention to agricultural and regional policies.

Future membership of the EC would put pressure on the heavily subsidized Finnish agriculture, with producer prices double those of the EC. It is believed that the agricultural sector could be reduced to half its size, in terms of both employed labour force and share of GNP. However, policy-makers believe structural changes will have to come, regardless of EC membership, through the conclusion of the Uruguay Round. Finland has an extensive regional policy, aimed at keeping remote areas populated for social, economic and security reasons. Its negotiating target is to gain understanding for the special living conditions in the north and to extend the provisions of the CAP and the regional policy to suit arctic areas.

The Finnish application sent to the Portuguese presidency in March 1992 is based on the shorter formula – that is, no reservation was made on neutrality. In his speech to the parliament the day before submitting the Finnish application, the Prime Minister underlined that Finland approved of the *acquis communautaire*, the content of the Treaty on EU and the *finalités politiques* of the Union. This implies that Finland has adjusted its concept of neutrality, but not abandoned it. The speech states:

> Finland has always pursued a policy aimed at stability and security in northern Europe. On the basis of our location and historical experience, neutrality is our aim in any armed

conflicts possibly arising in the proximity of Finland. The core of our policy of neutrality in today's Europe may be characterized as military non-alignment and an independent defence.

The Finnish position on CFSP and a possible future defence dimension of the Union is similar to the Swedish. Commentators are divided on the question of redefining the neutrality concept. Positions vary according to their views on the future situation in the CIS and whether the EC moves towards a common defence policy. The report presented to the parliament on the consequences of an EC membership[21] states that the position on security questions will be clarified during the negotiations. It is expected in Finland that the Commission in its Opinion on Finland's membership of the EU, due in October or November 1992, will propose the same conditions in the field of security and defence as it did in its Opinion on Swedish membership. There have been hints that Finland might ask for observer status in WEU, were it to become a member of the EU.[22]

It has been argued that the core of Finland's neutrality policy was based on pragmatism, in that its aim was to increase the country's freedom of action, as well as to be better situated as regards west European economic integration. Pragmatism would imply that it could be possible to abandon the neutrality policy if vital national interests so required. Another aim of Finnish neutrality was to prevent Finland from being embroiled as an ally of the Soviet Union in the event of a superpower conflict. The new definition of the neutrality concept retains this desire to stay out of any conflict where Russia could be the adversary. This line of thought puts stress not on the definition of neutrality, but on the continuity of the foreign policy. Membership of the EC would be compatible with Finnish foreign policy, but Finland, like other EC members, ought to have the right to pursue vital national interests.[23]

In the recent turmoil surrounding the ratification of the Treaty on EU, public opinion in Finland seems to have been less affected than in neighbouring Nordic countries. Recent figures show that

54% of the population still favour EC membership.[24] Prime Minister Aho welcomed the positive result in the French referendum on the treaty, because 'the outcome, as I see it, facilitates the launching of negotiations on the enlargement of the Community'.[25]

Iceland

Icelandic foreign policy in the post-war period has been based on two pillars: the transatlantic relationship and Nordic cooperation. Although a member of EFTA since 1970, Iceland is not to any great extent economically integrated with EFTA as a whole, and does not share the same interests in trade-related matters. For instance, it had to press hard for almost twenty years to make the other EFTA countries accept the principle of free trade in fishery products. The Icelandic government considers the EEA at this stage the only alternative to integration with the EC. The EEA gives Iceland the opportunity to pursue its traditional foreign and trade policy, and, at the same time, to take part in the internal market of the EEA, thus avoiding possible economic and political isolation. Jon Baldvin Hannibalsson, the Icelandic Foreign Minister, underlined this approach by stating that, for the moment, EC membership is not on the agenda, and that even if the EEA does not provide a place at the centre, it helps to avoid isolation to an extent which might be sufficient for a country with limited or circumscribed ambitions.[26]

Iceland's political life is conditioned by two features: its geographical position and its nearly total dependence on fishing resources as a source of national income. Iceland gained its independence from Denmark in 1944, and, being a young and small state, it guards attentively its sovereignty and national identity. Soon after the end of the Second World War, it had to make an important decision on whether or not to become a member of NATO in order to guarantee its national security. Iceland has no army of its own, and relies on the USA for military protection provided by strategically placed military bases.[27] In general, Icelandic politicians consider the tendency towards diminished American military presence in Europe an alarming development. There are worries that NATO might be replaced by a bilateral EC–US alliance within which the WEU would develop into the military arm of the Community. It is therefore feared that a small member country of NATO that is not a member of the EC might lose considerably in terms of real influence.

Its geographical position, far from the European continent, has made Iceland look across the Atlantic for export markets. Western Europe is in trade terms more important than North America, but Iceland is anyhow less dependent on European markets than the other EFTA countries.

The fishing industry plays a crucial role in Iceland's economy. Fish is the only natural resource that substantially contributes in terms of export earnings and employment. Iceland has categorically refused the principle of linkage between access to resources and access to markets on which the EC's common fisheries policy (CFP) is based. In the EEA negotiations, the Icelandic refusal to accept this principle – shared by the Norwegians – led to considerable difficulties. Finally, a deal was struck, partly in the EEA treaty whereby some fishing products were granted access to the EC markets, and partly on a bilateral basis, whereby the resource question was settled. The CFP is the main obstacle to Iceland joining the EC, because of both the competition for fishing grounds and the constraints on markets. The Foreign Minister stated that it might be possible to retain national control over resources were Iceland to become a member of the EC, but that this would depend on the goodwill of the EC member states and could be settled through tough accession negotiations. The Community's insistence on the strict observance of the *acquis communautaire* would make this difficult to achieve.

The question of EC membership has not yet been publicly discussed in Iceland.[28] The political parties and those segments of society that represent the anti-EC movement are either straightforwardly against the EEA and EC membership, or accept the EEA as the lesser evil. Recently, Icelandic industrialists have suggested that an EC membership application should be presented in order to register Iceland as a potential candidate. The proposition has not been endorsed by the government, but it is nevertheless clear that a change of mood is under way. Iceland fears that the second pillar of its foreign policy, the Nordic pillar, will be undermined by the Nordic candidate countries' preoccupation with their membership applications. Recent attempts to revive the old Hanseatic League among the countries around the Baltic Sea are viewed with suspicion by the Icelanders, who fear being left out of this cooperation. What could finally tilt the Icelandic decision on EC membership is a Norwegian application. It is a matter not just of cultural and historical links with a neighbour, but also of the dramatic effects on the Icelandic fishing industry were its most vigorous competitor to become a member of the EC. Norwegian fish products would enjoy preferential treatment and make the Community virtually self-sufficient in fish.

Iceland, together with Norway, the Faroe Islands and Greenland, has decided to set up a new organization, the North Atlantic Commission of Marine Mammals, to mobilize opposition to the International Whaling Commission's conservation policies. Iceland withdrew from the IWC as a result of its decision to authorize the commercial fishing of whales despite the IWC's ban. Both Norway and Iceland have been strongly criticized by the Commission, as well as by some member states, for their decision to take up whale fishing again.[29]

Iceland has so far adopted a strategy of wait and see concerning the possibility of EC membership. On the one hand, it is satisfied with what the EEA treaty grants in terms of political and economic influence in the European integration process. On the other hand, it would like to postpone a national debate on EC membership until developments show what shape the Community will take and how it deals with the challenge of enlargement.

Norway

The Norwegian case is special in that the country has already completed a round of membership negotiations with the EC. Accession failed after a hard and emotional debate leading up to a referendum in 1972, when the Norwegian electorate turned down the membership alternative by a narrow margin (47% in favour,

53% against). The question of EC membership subsequently fell by the wayside. It did not re-emerge as a factor in public debate until the end of 1991, although in parliament the debate had already started in 1988. Norway has often been regarded from the outside as the Nordic country closest to the EC because of its participation in the first enlargement negotiation and its membership of NATO. Norwegians, however, have often promoted the Atlantic dimension and oriented themselves westwards. The present situation is complex and has to be seen in the context of previous experience.

After the referendum of 1972, Norway remained a member of EFTA and negotiated a bilateral free trade agreement with the EC. During the 1980s, Norway became more enmeshed economically with the EC and dependent on its market. By 1990, nearly 60% of Norwegian exports went to the EC, compared with 22% to EFTA markets.[30] Therefore, Gro Harlem Brundtland, the Norwegian Prime Minister, replied positively to President Delors's initiative in 1989, in whose creation she had been involved,[31] to construct an enlarged European free trade area. For the government, the EEA offered a potential solution to square the circle of access to the internal market crucial to Norwegian industry, yet avoiding the difficult issue of EC membership. The restricted integration inherent in the EEA has nevertheless stirred the political debate and to a certain extent brought back the arguments of 1972. On the whole, the government has succeeded in keeping the political situation in hand.

The economy is an important factor in shaping Norwegian society and relations with the EC. The dominant trend over the past twenty years is dependence on oil and gas revenues, which have allowed the country to pursue an independent economic policy. On the other hand, Norwegian industry has become increasingly less diversified, which makes it harder to absorb shocks to the economy resulting from fluctuating oil prices. Indeed, some Norwegian industrialists are deeply worried about the structural weaknesses of their industrial base.

The oil economy influences the EC debate in two directions: the anti-EC movements argue that the country's freedom of economic manoeuvre, made possible by the oil and gas revenues, would be curtailed by EC membership. Conversely, the pro-EC groups advocate the need to diversify Norwegian industry and to expose it to international competition by gaining access to the internal market. Norway's oil and gas resources would give the country a strong position if and when it starts negotiating with the EC on accession. Norway, were it to become a member of the EC, would play a central role in shaping EC policies in the fields of energy and shipping.

Behind these arguments lie important economic and political considerations. Regional policy is designed to give financial support to remote areas in order to attract industry and to preserve the social infrastructure and pattern of economic activity in the north. Norwegian agriculture is dependent on financial support from regional funds in order to remain in its present form. The groups favoured by the regional measures are represented administratively and politically by their respective districts (Norway is divided into districts on a geographical basis). The districts play an important role in Norwegian political life and therefore provide a forum for regional interests to make their voices heard. The northern districts, in particular, draw on popular support in their efforts to protect the interests of these groups.

The party which represents farmers and other regional interests in parliament, the Centre Party, is against any move towards closer cooperation with the EC. It is joined by the Socialist Left Party, which represents a mix of intellectual city dwellers and white- and blue-collar workers in urban and rural areas. In the referendum of 1972, the country was broadly split down an urban/rural divide. (This is somewhat simplified, since there was also division between age groups, language groups, Christian and populist movements, etc.) Recent trends show, however, that groups in society which were previously loyal to the farmers' claims are now less ready to give them support. There are trends showing that the rural/urban divide might well become a north/south divide, in which economic and regional interests will have an important impact. Polarized interests are captured in party politics and parliamentary debates. Some parties, like the Centre Party, show a marked increase in popular support when the EC question is debated because of the strong interest the question evokes among certain groups in society. The EC debate has again become emotionally heated and revolves around issues such as loss of sovereignty and national identity, as well as protection of the environment and maintaining the regional policy.

If Norway decides to take part in accession negotiations, certain substantial areas will be very sensitive: fisheries, agricultural and regional policies, with farmers and fishermen fearing the changes a membership might bring and therefore demanding that the government try to negotiate for a certain level of financial support; energy policy, where the principle of Community access to resources might be difficult for Norwegians to accept. Commentators believe that the actual outcome of the accession negotiations on substantive issues would be fundamental to the Norwegian population's acceptance of EC membership. But events such as the Danish and French referenda, as well as the conflict over whaling between Norway and Iceland, on one hand, and the IWC on the other, supported by Commissioner Marin and several MEPs, are bound to influence public opinion.

The key political factor in the debate on the EEA and EC membership is the ruling party, the Labour Party. In 1972, the party was divided on the EC question and lost more votes that any other in subsequent general elections. Its leader, Prime Minister Brundtland, is being careful not to repeat the same mistakes. Last time, the party was criticized for having taken the decision to seek membership of the EC without prior consultation with either the party grassroots or the population as a whole.

The Prime Minister is consequently pursuing her own strategy and timetable. Officially, she had wanted the EEA treaty ratified in parliament before the membership debate could start, but, since the conclusion of the EEA was delayed, she decided to declare her personal view on the membership question at a regional party meeting in April 1992. As expected, this meeting presented the Prime Minister with an occasion to come out in favour of Norway seeking membership of the EC.[32] This pro-Europe standpoint was endorsed by eight regional branches of the party, while only the one farthest to the north, Nordland, remained hostile because of its interests in the fishing and agricultural sectors.

The Labour Party will continue to discuss the question at all levels right up to the party conference in November 1992, when it will announce its formal position. The party's position on EC membership would seem to be firmly endorsed, since the regional meeting in April also elected delegates to the national conference, of whom 60% were in favour of presenting an application to the EC. It is widely expected that they will vote in favour of the government presenting an application to the EC presidency in November. The pro-EC groups hope for grassroots support for membership, enabling the Labour Party to stand on firm ground in the difficult EC debate. Despite all efforts to reach party unity on the question, however, many members remain negative or unconvinced that EC membership is good for Norway, which leaves the field open to attacks on the Prime Minister's policy.

A recent government reshuffle resulted in the replacement of six ministers and a change of post for three others. Since then all ministers, notably of Foreign Affairs, Environment and Finance, support the Prime Minister's position on EC membership – but some more than others. One of the Prime Minister's strongest supporters, Gunnar Berge, was given the ministerial portfolio for regional policy. In order to ward off a split in the party over the EC, the fisheries ministry is now headed by Jan Henry T. Olson.[33] He has endorsed the government's EC policy, but remains somewhat sceptical on the grounds that membership of the EC could ruin the whole Norwegian fishing industry. None the less, he has also expressed the conviction that failure to adopt the EEA treaty would bring the same result.[34]

During summer and early autumn 1992, the political parties started to position themselves on the question of EEA ratification and EC membership. The first battleground was the vote on the EEA treaty, which was adopted by parliament on 16 October 1992 by a majority of 130 to 35. The bill, which needed a 75% majority to pass, received support from the Labour Party, the Conservatives, the Christian Peoples' Party and the Progress Party, while primarily MPs from the Centre Party and the Socialist Left Party voted against.

During autumn 1992, the Prime Minister was much disturbed by unofficial discussion among some members of the Labour Party and the anti-EC Socialist Left Party about the possibility of alliance at the next general election in 1993. The Prime Minister, who denied the possibility of such an alliance, was determined to brush off what seemed to be an internal challenge to her leadership.[35] The Socialist Left Party has decided, along the same lines as the Centre Party, not necessarily to respect a positive outcome of a future referendum on a Norwegian membership of the EC. The party advocates the adoption of a system similar to that of the Swiss (which requires a double majority of regions and voters) in order to strengthen the power of the regions.[36] The Centre Party has announced its intention to withdraw Norway's application for membership if it should form a government with other anti-EC parties after the 1993 general election.[37]

The Conservative Party, the largest opposition party, are strongly in favour of EC membership (although also among the Conservatives there are some – notably from rural areas – who oppose it). Their positive attitude towards the EC caused the break-up of the right-wing coalition government in the late 1980s, since the junior coalition partner, the Centre Party, dissented. The Conservative leader, Kaci Kulleman Five, has strongly advocated Norwegian membership of the EC inside and outside parliament, but has also conscientiously respected the government's strategy in order not to upset the efforts to prepare for a balanced debate.

External events have influenced the Norwegian debate, which for a long time was characterized by attachment to the status quo. First, the break-up of the Soviet Union has altered the security situation in northern Norway. Norway, which has been a faithful member of NATO and has a consultative link with European Political Cooperation (EPC), is prudently following up the invitation to seek associate membership in WEU, offered by the European Council at Maastricht. Second, some groups have realized that the EEA might not be more than an intermediate solution to EC membership. The limited influence on the decision-making process is deemed unsatisfactory. Finally, the policies of Nordic neighbours, in particular the Swedish and Finnish membership applications, have had some impact on the Norwegian public. The prospect of being left as the only mainland Nordic country outside the EC is viewed with apprehension; a Nordic bloc within an enlarged EC might seem less threatening to national identity and sovereignty.

However, the negative result in the Danish referendum in June had a clear effect on the debates over both EEA and EC membership and public attitudes. After a period of evenly divided views, a June opinion poll reflected 49% opposing Norwegian EC membership, with 35% in favour and 16% undecided. The polls also showed a slide in Labour party support (down to 25.7%), with the Conservative Party also losing in popularity. The Centre Party and the Socialist Left Party somewhat increased their popularity among the voters.[38] The Prime Minister retained her positive position on Norwegian membership of the EC, stating that 'Denmark's rejection of the EC Union will not affect Norway's wish to be where the political decisions will be made which will influence the future of Europe ... Norway's interests are closely connected to those of the rest of Europe and the EC, and this situation has not been changed by the result of the referendum in Denmark'.[39]

The Prime Minister also expressed satisfaction with the narrow 'yes' in the French referendum on the EU treaty, but underlined that she saw no direct impact on a Norwegian application for membership, since the Norwegians would themselves first have to decide whether or not to apply.[40] The previous trend in the electorate that had coupled support for parties with their official positions on EC membership now seems to have been broken. In a September poll, the support for EC membership fell further, to 32%, while opposition reached 44%. Another poll measuring party popularity, however, indicated that the Labour Party has regained ground, with 30% support, a recovery by the Conservative Party

and the anti-EC parties falling back.[41] The debate on EC membership continues to be an issue on which political parties can both lose
and gain votes.

Sweden

Sweden was the first of the Nordic countries in EFTA to make a
decisive step towards the Community, when it presented its
membership application in June 1991. The Social Democratic government's decision to seek membership was the culmination of a
fundamental shift in Swedish politics. The party's attitude towards
the Community was from the 1950s characterized by an ideological
scepticism on European integration and a conviction that the EC
was not the right forum for developing the Swedish welfare model.
In addition, Swedish neutrality was found to be incompatible with
membership, though the Social Democratic government came
close to applying in the late 1960s.

Signs of change appeared in the late 1980s, when the government and the leading social partners welcomed integration into the
attractive internal European market through the creation of the
EEA. In late 1990, the Swedish parliament endorsed by an overwhelming majority the government's decision that 'Sweden shall
apply for membership of the EC with the retention of neutrality'.[42]
The strong parliamentary majority left it to the government to
choose how and when it would present the application. When the
formal application was handed to the Dutch presidency the following summer, the Swedish request for membership was reduced to
one sentence and no special point was made on neutrality.

The reorientation was prompted by rapid change in the political
context in Europe, new conditions in the global economy and a
slow, if less spectacular, shift in Swedish political life. Since the
mid-1980s, Sweden has quietly adapted national legislation to EC
requirements.[43] As a step towards voluntary integration into the
Community, monetary policy was deregulated. The freeing of
capital resulted in a large outflow of money and Sweden became a
net exporter of capital in the late 1980s. Since Swedish companies
preferred to invest abroad, jobs were no longer being created in the

country. Swedish industry was becoming an integrated part of the European internal market, while the country still remained outside.

The Social Democratic Party, which was in power almost uninterruptedly from 1932 to 1991, was torn by diverging views on whether formally to integrate with the EC or not. It was also weakened in parliament by its position as a minority government. A conflict fought within the party between the groups for and against European integration was worsened by a sluggish economy and strikes. The Prime Minister, Ingvar Carlsson, and his government had to resign in the winter of 1990 after a battle over an austerity programme. Since the opposition refused to take over, the government, somewhat reorganized, resumed office. But it had lost its credibility and scored all-time low results in the national opinion polls.

During the following economic crises, the forces for change in the Social Democratic Party took over, and, significantly, the government announced its intention to pursue a policy of rapprochement to the EC, presented briefly as a point in an economic austerity package. The decision was made possible by the shift in position of the central trade union, which now favoured EC membership.

The right-wing parties, with the exception of the Centre Party, have for several years been in favour of EC membership. The outcome of the election in September 1991 produced a four-party coalition government, led by the Conservative Party leader, Carl Bildt. The government is forcefully pursuing Sweden's membership application and is eager to start negotiating as soon as possible. It is determined, with the support of the Social Democratic party, to retain a fixed exchange-rate policy and to exclude devaluation. The aim is to prove that the krona is fit to enter the ERM and that Sweden is ready to meet the convergence criteria of the EMU. The September 1992 currency crisis paved the way for an emergency economic package, agreed with the Social Democrats and based on the eradication of the budgetary deficit through tax increases and cuts in welfare benefits. In the long term, the agreement could lead to a radical change in the financing of the Swedish welfare system. The economic difficulties that were already troubling the Social Democratic government at the end of the 1980s worsened during 1992, despite the efforts of the new government to curb the budget deficit and to reduce large public-sector spending by introducing radical reforms. The economic crisis has resulted in an increase in unemployment and a fall in industrial output, giving rise to public worries about the dismantling of the Swedish welfare system. This downward economic trend is often confused with the government's efforts to adapt to EC membership. When the currency crisis broke in September, the Swedish Central Bank raised the marginal interest rate to 75%, in order to protect the krona and stop the outflow of capital, and then on 16 September to the unprecedented level of 500%.[44]

The official Swedish position on EC membership is a total acceptance of the *acquis communautaire* and *politique*, which implies that Sweden accepts totally the plans towards a fully implemented CFSP. The government has not ruled out any option, including observer status or membership of WEU, once Sweden is a member of the EC. This would imply a radical reformulation of Sweden's defence policy. Thus far, the government's position has been that Sweden ought to keep an independent national army to defend its borders, which might, as has been the case in several UN-supported missions, be involved in future peacekeeping activities outside Sweden. The government argues that it is difficult to give concrete answers to specific questions until the Community has developed further the shape of its future security and defence structure. In the wake of events in central and eastern Europe, the neutrality concept has been redefined as 'non-alignment to military organizations'.[45]

The change may not be so very extraordinary in that the application of Swedish neutrality has historically been pragmatic. Neutrality was easier to define during the cold war, when the world was divided between two military blocs; but today, some groups argue, it has become obsolete. In 1992 the Foreign Affairs committee adopted new guidelines for Swedish security policy, on the ground that the end of the cold war has created new conditions for Europe and the world at large. The committee drew three conclusions from this: first, the term 'neutrality' no longer adequately described the foreign and security policy that Sweden wanted to pursue, which should have a true European identity; second, Sweden, along with other European nations, had a vital interest in taking part in the building of a new security structure in Europe in order to manage, control and solve tensions and threats to stability; and, third, Sweden alone had responsibility for defending by sea or air its large territory in the strategically important area between the North Atlantic Sea and northeastern Russia.[46]

All the parliamentary parties, except the former Communist Party, which now calls itself the Left Party, are in favour of membership. There is a broad consensus that Sweden should play an active and constructive part in the EC. The debate on EC membership has begun to show signs of taking a more traditional party-political turn as specific interests start to crystallize. The Social Democratic Party plans its own yes-campaign, separate from the government's, in the run-up to a referendum on EC membership. The Greens, which lost their representation in parliament in the 1991 election, are strongly against membership. One of their spokesmen, Per Garthon, has publicly argued against the EC and is a leading figure in the growing anti-EC movement. He argues that Sweden would have little influence as a member of EU, that Swedish democracy would be eroded and the policy of neutrality would have to be abandoned.[47]

Swedish officials have anticipated very few substantive problems in the negotiations with the EC. The Commission presented its Opinion on Sweden's application in late July 1992.[48] This underlined again an insistence on the *acquis* of EU. The Union, according to the Commission, 'will on the whole benefit from accession of Sweden, which would widen the circle of countries whose prospective economic, monetary and budgetary performance is likely to contribute to the development of the Economic and Monetary Union ... Sweden's record in democratic tradition and human rights are as valid as her important place in European history and culture.' The Commission stressed the importance of the EEA treaty, which already requires that the *acquis* of the internal market has to be adopted.

Problems might arise in some areas, such as the agricultural sector, the state monopoly for alcoholic beverages and the regional policy, but the Commission expects these to be resolvable during the accession negotiations.

Swedish farmers are largely in favour of joining the EC, with the exception of those living in the north, who fear that national regional support would no longer be allowed within the EU. Traditionally, Swedish farmers were as heavily subsidized as those in the other Nordic countries, but in the late 1980s the Social Democratic government introduced a programme of restructuring. This programme aims to reduce overproduction and to introduce market-guided conditions for the farmers. The reform would abolish some traditional measures which still form an integral part of the CAP, and might therefore have to be reintroduced. Farmers in Sweden are, however, worried more by exclusion from the CAP than by the prospect of lower prices and a higher level of competition inside the Community. Were Sweden a member of the EC, Swedish farmers would – through the CAP – regain a great deal of the support that they are losing under the Swedish reform.[49]

Both Commissioners Andriessen and Millan have declared that there would be no problems about retaining regional support for northern Sweden. How the provisions would be worked out is a matter for resolution during the accession negotiations, but the chances of introducing measures for 'arctic farming' are good.[50] In any case, regional policy poses less of a problem for Sweden than for the other Nordic countries, since a smaller proportion of the Swedish population lives in the north.

In the area of CFSP, the Commission noted that 'Swedish policy has evolved significantly', but also that 'Sweden will be required to accept and be able to implement this policy [CFSP] as it evolves'. The Commission pointed out that 'there seem to remain reservations in the Swedish position relative to the eventual framing of a common defence policy and, in a more marked way, regarding the possible establishment of a common defence'. It recommended that 'specific and binding assurances from Sweden should be sought with regard to her political commitment and legal capacity to fulfil the obligations in this area'.

Swedish reactions to the Commission's Opinion were generally positive. Many commentators saw the Opinion as a document endorsing Sweden's suitability to become a member of EU. As regards the 'specific and binding assurances' of the commitment to a common defence, the Minister of Europe, Ulf Dinkelspiel, stated that defence policy is an open question among the EC members and that Sweden could not be asked to go further. He added that it seems clear that the Union will develop a defence dimension, but that the decision will not be taken before 1996.[51] It has been suggested that the legitimate conditions for the Community to ask of Sweden in the accession negotiations are that it should agree to existing political objectives and not block any agreement or action relating to these. The specific and binding assurances that the Commission considered necessary should be interpreted as a means of dealing with Austrian and Swiss neutralities, which reside on legal foundations, and not the Swedish, which is not limited by any international, constitutional or legalistic provisions.[52]

A major hurdle in the Swedish position is the time-frame in which the negotiations are going to take place. EC membership would require changes in the Swedish constitution, which have to be endorsed by two successive parliaments with a general election in between. The negotiation result will have to be presented nine months in advance to the parliament before the first decision can be taken. On the Swedish side, it is therefore hoped that the negotiations will be finished by December 1993 in time to be presented to and endorsed by the current parliament. In 1994, there would then be both a general election and a referendum on EC membership. The new parliament would then be able to endorse the decision taken in 1993. Sweden's position might make it sensitive to delays in opening informal negotiations, as well as to prolonged formal accession negotiations.

The Swedish public have generally favoured EC membership. However, as the debate becomes more specific, groups with particular interests have started to voice their worries. The Danish no-vote in the referendum on the Treaty on EU had a strong impact on Swedish public opinion. The anti-EC movements saw their cause justified, since the arguments against EU are very similar in the two countries. An opinion poll in September 1992, asking whether people believed membership would be accepted in the referendum planned for 1994, revealed 43% expected EC membership would be accepted, and slightly over 41% thought it would be rejected. Only 16% were undecided.[53] Another poll measuring public support for the Swedish membership application revealed that only 28% were in favour and as many as 45% against. This poll also showed signs that the Swedish Social Democratic Party might face the same problem as the Norwegian Labour Party in rallying their voters to support membership: of the Social Democratic supporters asked, 47% were against entry to the EC and 24% in favour.[54]

Various anti-EC movements have been established, representing, for example, women in the public sector, who fear they will lose their jobs if Sweden were to become a member of the EC, or Green groups, which are concerned that Sweden would not be able to maintain its high level of environmental protection. Criticism is also heard on the loss of sovereignty and the undemocratic features of the EC structure. In general, many people are bewildered by the speed with which the political elite has changed its position as regards the EC and the short period of time between the positive statement in parliament and the submission of an application to the EC. The social partners, however, have influenced and paved the way for a swift shift in public opinion towards membership by launching an extensive information campaign in order to raise public awareness about the Community.

Switzerland

Switzerland, with its central position in Europe, four language groups and unique political system, has always seen itself as a *Sonderfall*, a special case. It is true the Swiss have shared the history of the continent with other Europeans, but at the same time, they have been careful to keep away from any deep political involvement. In 1991, as the Swiss Confederation celebrated its 700 years of existence, it also had to confront a new set of issues which might have considerable implications for the country. The Federal Council decided to seek membership of the EC in May 1992.

Switzerland, one of the founding members of EFTA, signed a bilateral free trade agreement with the EC in 1972. Relations have been extended since then through a gradual and pragmatic process, aiming at closer cooperation with the Community. For Switzerland, as well as for the other EFTA states, the break-through in the relationship with the EC came in 1989, with the launching of the EEA initiative. Eventually, after having tried to keep its approach to the EC on a bilateral and pragmatic basis, Switzerland welcomed the EEA approach, since it offered a systematic and multilateral form of integration with the Community and an access to rapid developments in the internal market. It noted that, in order to follow developments in the European integration process, only two alternatives were sufficiently far-reaching: membership of the EC or the EEA. Until October 1991, Switzerland preferred the latter approach as more likely to take account of its institutional, economic and social organization.[55] At the same time, the Federal Council stated that it was important not to lose sight of the possibility of EC membership, in case the EEA negotiations were to result in an unsatisfactory institutional set-up. It also listed a series of events that, irrespective of the outcome of the EEA process, could cause the Federal Council to reconsider submitting an application for EC membership:[56]

> A situation in Europe where East/West antagonism has vanished completely and a new European architecture is emerging in which the EC plays an important role; new enlargements of the Community; strengthening of the ten-

dency of demanding non-EC members to cooperate on the basis of a harmonization of their legislation to the one prevailing in the Community; affirmation of the federal approach in the EC and a systematic application of the subsidiarity principle and that the Community comes to play a considerably more important role at the world level.

The negotiations over the EEA soon proved more difficult than had been expected by the participants. In the beginning of the process, the EFTA countries had hoped to persuade the EC to accept permanent derogations in certain areas. When it became clear that this would not be possible, and that the EFTA countries would not be granted decisive influence in the decision-shaping process, the enthusiasm of the Federal Council faltered. Its response was clear: if the negotiations could not result in an acceptable outcome, especially on the institutional question, the Council would not sign the treaty, nor would it propose ratification.[57] The Council concluded that, given Switzerland's 'European vocation' and its desire to take part in building the new Europe, recent events had made the option of seeking EC membership a serious proposition. It added that although there was no reason for a precipitate decision, the option was now on the agenda.

In October 1991, when the outcome of the EEA negotiations was politically endorsed by the ministerial meeting between the EC and the EFTA states, the Swiss Federal Council for the first time declared its intention eventually to seek membership of the EC. On several occasions, including in March 1992, the President of the Swiss Confederation, René Felber, reconfirmed the Federal Council's intention by stating that the accession to the EC had become the objective of its integration policy, but that the date of submitting the application remained open. The EEA was an important step towards this objective and would permit Switzerland to adapt its internal economic structures to the internal market.[58]

The Federal Council's positive approach towards further integration opened the debate on possible membership of the EC. The groups in favour of membership argue that, given Switzerland's geographical position and its dependence on trade with the EC, it is not possible to stay outside an integrated Community market. The EEA provides access to this market, but by extending obligations, and by conceding only some rights in terms of real influence in the decision-making process and balance between the institutions of the EC and EFTA. Already the EEA is triggering difficult constitutional and political adjustments. Some groups have therefore argued that Switzerland should take the opportunity now to become a member and thus be able to take part in shaping the Community's future.

The anti-EC groups believe that integration with the EC would undermine the basic principles of the Confederation, namely the system of direct democracy, Swiss federalism and the credibility of Swiss neutrality. The EEA to a certain extent regulates some areas which these groups want to protect: the freedom of movement of workers, the right for EEA citizens to buy Swiss property, and, in part, the contentious questions of transport and banking; they consider that acceptance of the *acquis communautaire* and *politique* would not only put these areas at risk, but jeopardize Swiss national identity.[59] Swiss farmers are not worried about the implications of the EEA, since it does not cover the agricultural sector. By contrast, they are strongly against eventual EC membership in that they would stand to lose a great deal if they were to switch from the current system of price and income support to the CAP. The consequences, however, might be less disastrous than is assumed at present, since the CAP is about to undergo a major reform which would favour income support instead of price support. It is also widely assumed that the Swiss agricultural sector would have to change the base of its support regardless of possible membership of the EC, and that this might be more easily brought about by accession.

The anti-EC groups believed for a time that *Alleingang*, going-it-alone, would be a better alternative for Switzerland as a whole, and in practical terms a plausible one, since Switzerland would be able to negotiate a bilateral agreement with the EC if the other alternatives were to fail. The opponents include groups on both the right and the left which, for different motives, oppose EC member-ship and/or the EEA. In combination they could lead to an unholy alliance and become a problem for ratification through the referen-dum which is required for the EEA, as well as for Community membership.

Switzerland's economy is heavily integrated with that of the EC. In 1991, 58.8% of Swiss exports went to the Community, while 70.2% of imports came from the member countries.[60] This means that Switzerland is the EC's second largest trading partner after the USA and before Japan. Consequently, the industrial interest groups are largely in favour of both the EEA and eventual EC membership. The Swiss political system is based on two guiding principles: direct democracy and federalism. Membership of the EC would require adaptation of both these principles and would entail certain competences, especially of the Confederation, being transferred to the Community level. In addition, Switzerland would have to adapt its system of indirect taxation. On the whole, Switzerland's accession would be made easier if the principle of subsidiarity came to be thoroughly implemented in the EC.

The Swiss constitution distinguishes clearly between federal and cantonal competences, stating that the cantons 'are sovereign in so far as their sovereignty is not limited by the Federal constitu-tion'. Integration with the Community would affect matters which are mainly federal competencies and would not require a formal transfer of power from the cantons to the federation. Cantons would be able to exercise some powers within the framework of EC or EEA regulations. They could retain a great deal of manoeuvre with regard to the implementation of EC or EEA law, keeping in mind that many directives set up the objective which has to be achieved and leaves the mode of implementation to be chosen by the member states. It has even been suggested that EEA and EC membership could strengthen, not weaken, federal ties inside Switzerland, since the cantons would have to be more involved in exchanges of information and consultation in order to prepare Swiss positions on decisions taken at Community level.[61]

Direct democracy is based on a system of referenda and initiatives. Any bill adopted by the Federal Assembly must be submitted to a referendum if a petition, bearing the signature of 50,000 citizens, is submitted within a period of 90 days. A popular initiative signed by 100,000 citizens, aiming at amending or revising the constitution, has to be submitted to a referendum. An initiative has to be approved by a double majority, i.e. both by the population as a whole and by the cantons. Theoretically, the signing of the EEA treaty will not reduce any of these features of direct democracy, but it would be politically difficult if the result were to produce conflict with responsibilities under an international treaty. The EEA treaty contains a suspension clause which would come into force if any one EFTA country was to refuse any specific EEA directive. Such an outcome would have an adverse impact on Switzerland and on other EFTA countries, as well as on the EEA as a whole.

The institutional balance between the Federal Council and the Federal Assembly will change in favour of the former with the entry into force of the EEA treaty. The Council, composed of seven members from the main political parties, would represent Switzerland in the institutional framework of the EEA. A major reorganization of the Federal Council is in the process of being prepared to take account of EC membership responsibilities and work load.[62] The Federal Assembly, however, would lose its right to legislate in the areas covered by provisions of direct applicability to the EEA treaty, and in the future would be confined to the implementation of the directives.

The Swiss form of neutrality would be at issue in a negotiation for membership of the Community. It reflects the differences among the population in terms of culture, language and religion, and has been, in a sense, a domestic necessity to prevent the splitting of the confederation by minority groups tempted to ally with strong neighbours to the north, west and south. It is therefore understandable that neutrality has become a uniting factor and a national symbol in Switzerland.

But the rapid developments in Europe did not pass unnoticed in Switzerland. With the end of the cold war, the Swiss have begun to recognize the need to redefine neutrality so as better to reflect the reality of Europe today. An expert group set up by the Federal Council published a report on neutrality. It advocated a more restricted interpretation of neutrality, basically reducing it to military neutrality in an armed conflict, and thus presenting no contradiction between neutrality and membership of the EC in its present form. Problems would then arise only if the EC developed a common defence policy. The Minister of Defence, Kaspar Villiger, defined the various categories of conflict in which Switzerland would remain neutral: for example, a conflict between European states or between third parties far from Europe. But, if the European democracies were threatened by an external force, Switzerland would participate loyally in the defence of the continent.[63]

Since 18 May 1992, the official government policy has been to pursue EC membership. The Federal Council had debated since November 1991 when, rather than whether, to submit a Swiss application, some government ministers having wanted to apply before the EEA referendum on 6 December 1992, some after. It was stressed on several occasions that there was no necessary link between the referendum and the submission of a membership application. But it was clear that the Federal Council was concerned lest a negative outcome in the referendum on the EEA (which requires double majority, i.e. of the cantons and the population as a whole) might block further rapprochement to the EC. Now it can argue that the two, i.e. EC membership and the EEA, are not directly related.

A rejection of the EEA treaty in the referendum would, nevertheless, have a negative impact on the aim of EC membership. It was therefore a great relief to the government when a referendum on 27 September 1992 on the two rail tunnels, a requirement of the bilateral agreement on transit between the EC and Switzerland, was endorsed by a comfortable majority (63.5%) in favour. The agreement on transit was a compromise struck after hard negotiation on the EEA, since Switzerland and Austria had refused to accept full free movement of road transport. Although Swiss voters will have to pay £15bn for the whole project, they accepted it as a necessary measure for the implementation of the EEA. Analysts interpret the result as a good sign for the 6 December referendum on the EEA treaty.

There is some difference in attitudes to EC membership between the French– and the German–speaking regions, depending on their geographical position in relation to the country's borders. If the German cantons, which are in a majority, were to vote against the EEA treaty, it would lead to some tension with the French cantons.[64] The same applies to the EC membership question. The Federal Council's decision has received strong support in the French-speaking region, whereas in the German-speaking part there is some suspicion.[65] On the other hand, it can also be argued that any such differing tendencies in minority groups' preferences can be more easily absorbed in a confederal system such as that of the Swiss. The Swiss cantons have after all been intimately linked to each other for 700 years, approximately 550 years longer than the Swiss constitution has been in existence.

3.2 The central and east European countries

Virtually all of the new democracies of central and eastern Europe (CEE) have declared their intention of seeking membership of the EC in due course. In part, this signals a clear desire to be inside, not outside, the family of European democracies. It also connotes a belief that this will increase their leverage in the EC and improve their security position. The governments of the CEE countries understandably want as definite a commitment as they can get from the EC and its members that there will be sustained west European support for their economic and political transformation. They want their economies to be within the EC's regulatory framework and subject to its market incentives.

So far, however, EC policy has been to indicate that there is a hierarchy of relationships with the CEE countries – trade and cooperation agreements, Europe Agreements and only then the possibility of full membership. The Visegrad Three – the CSFR, Hungary and Poland – are furthest along this road, having already negotiated the Europe Agreements, which are scheduled for implementation in 1993, and being among the most advanced in terms of domestic transformation. After much initial resistance from some EC members, the Europe Agreements contain a reference to the possibility of eventual membership.

Bulgaria and Romania are negotiating for Europe Agreements, with Bulgaria expected to sign an agreement in late 1992. Thus these five democracies could then regard themselves as fast improving their eligibility for membership.

The questions which follow are when such 'Europe associates' might be expected to apply for full membership and what policy the EC should adopt towards them. CEE governments tend to say they want membership 'as soon as possible' and to have a timetable for accession in view. This constitutes a key plank in their foreign policies, but it is also framed in the hope that tabled applications will put pressure on the EC to implement the Europe Agreements in a more generous spirit. The Hungarian government has been the most impatient to apply early. By and large, CEE governments have so far been advised by their EC counterparts to let the Europe Agreements come into force first and begin to deliver results. The Visegrad Three, in contrast to the EFTA countries, are pursuing a joint policy towards the Community as regards future membership. They pledged closer cooperation between themselves and the EC and a clearer programme concerning their future membership of the Community.[66] This was spelled out in a joint memorandum presented in October 1992 to the EC foreign ministers by the governments of the Visegrad Three:

> Our three countries are convinced that stable democracy, respect for human rights and continued policy of economic reforms will make accession possible. We call upon the Communities and the member states to respond to our efforts by clearly stating the integration of our economies and societies, leading to membership of the Communities, is the aim of the Communities themselves. This simple, but historic statement would provide the anchor which we need.

The CSFR

The three Visegrad countries none the less face economic and political difficulties. Most spectacular is the decision of June 1992 to split the CSFR. The Federation was created in 1918 as a result of the Versailles peace agreement. Although forming two distinct cultural and economic communities, the Czechs and the Slovaks shared governance up to the Second World War, when Czechoslovakia was split up. The Czechs came under direct German rule, and the Slovaks enjoyed semi-independence through the creation of a Slovak Republic under strong German influence. In 1945, the Czechoslovak Republic was restored, but only three years later a communist regime took over. In 1989, the 'velvet revolution' erupted simultaneously in Prague and Bratislava, forming the basis for a new governing generation, with Vaclav Havel being elected overwhelmingly as president by both Czechs and Slovaks.[67]

None the less, the issue of the partition of the Federation came to be strongly debated in the run-up to the general election of June 1992. While the Czech political parties showed signs of following a more west European pattern of parties, with a spectrum of left- to right-wing views on economic matters and social reforms, the Slovak political debate was much influenced by the nationalist Movement for Democratic Slovakia led by Vladimir Meciar. Although Meciar was cautious not to propose a full partition of the Republic, he wanted a declaration of Slovak sovereignty, and the introduction of a constitution and a separate president for the Slovak republic.[68] The outcome of the general election left Vaclav Klaus to form a Czech government and Vladimir Meciar to form a government in Slovakia. In the troubled weeks that followed the election, the two leaders finally agreed to prepare the splitting of the Czech and Slovak Federal Republic into two separate states.

The Czech and Slovak leaders have engaged in talks on how to manage the split of the Federation. The plans involve the creation of a currency union, tariff-free movement of goods and visa-free movement of people. Other contentious issues, such as the partition of state property, the role of the army and military assets, and the coordination of foreign and security policy, await further discussion. In a vote in the federal parliament in early October 1992, the opposition parties rejected a government proposal for a constitutional division into two republics, and demanded a referendum to decide the issue. This move implies that the clean and speedy partition process that the two leading parties had hoped for will be delayed. They now have to seek a compromise solution with the opposition parties, which might prove to be both a difficult and a lengthy process.[69]

A fundamental difficulty lies in the different economic prospects of the two republics. The Czech lands under the leadership of Klaus have engaged in radical economic reforms, which already have resulted in foreign investment and make EC membership look credible in a not-too-distant future. The Czech economy is more diversified than the Slovak and its products are more easily exported. As a result, the rate of unemployment in the Czech lands stands at only 3% of the population. The Slovak economy, which relies to a great extent on arms production and other heavy industries, has been harder hit, and unemployment is currently running at nearly 12%. Economic restructuring is made more difficult because little investment capital can be attracted, and the prospect of privatizing the large state-owned industries is bleak. After a partition, the Slovaks would stand to lose Czech subsidies of between $300m and $1bn annually. The Slovaks also inherit two major international problems: the dispute with Hungary over the Danube river hydroelectric complex; and the Kivoi Rog iron ore enrichment project in Ukraine.[70] Slovakia, which has a large Hungarian minority (12% of the population), has an increasingly tense relationship with Hungary. The Slovak constitution, adopted in September, worsened the situation by not making provisions for the rights of ethnic minorities.

Questions therefore arise as to what will happen to the Europe Agreement previously negotiated between the EC and the CSFR. The Czech side is largely satisfied with retaining existing terms, while the Slovak side, more vulnerable to anti-dumping measures against its steel industry and to the loss of former financial subsidies from Prague, has a desperate need to gain freer access to EC markets.[71] These developments cause some problems for the EC. So far, EC policy-makers have worked hard to avoid inflaming divisions between Czechs and Slovaks, and have stressed that any adaptation of the Europe Agreement cannot be discussed until the position within the country has been clarified.

Poland
Poland experienced two months of political crises in 1992, following the collapse of Jan Olszewski's government after a six-month power struggle between him and the President, Lech Walesa. The conflict reached its climax when Prime Minister Olszewski decided to confront Poland's leading politicians and civil servants, including the President, with allegations of their past collaboration with the communist regime. In the event, he found himself outvoted in parliament by 273 votes to 119.[72] The next Prime Minister, Waldemar Pawlak, whose candidature had been supported by the President, had to resign after only a month in office. In July 1992, eight of the political parties represented in parliament agreed to propose Hanna Suchocka as their joint candidate. Hanna Suchocka, with the President's assent, formed a coalition government composed of parties emanating from the anti-communist Solidarity movement. Prime Minister Suchocka announced that the new government would give priority to the economic crisis in public finance, speed up privatization, raise efficiency in the state sector of the economy and modernize the agricultural sector.[73]

Parliament also voted in August 1992 for a constitutional reform, in an effort to settle the long-standing power conflict between the President and the government, which has caused political instability, delayed economic reforms and discouraged foreign investment. The amended constitution will enable the government to adopt economic measures without going through certain lengthy parliamentary procedures. The President will have a stronger role in forming new governments, but less power to dismiss them. Public discontent caused by frequent political crises and governmental inefficiency in dealing with the difficult economic situation made parliament realize that constitutional reform was essential.[74]

This political turmoil in Poland has not diminished its wish to forge closer links with the western states. On the contrary, President Walesa has confirmed that Poland's long-term aim is 'full integration with the North Atlantic Alliance and the European Union'.[75]

Hungary

Hungary, which had already in 1989 a fairly open economic structure, has come a long way in its reform process. The country is now struggling to reduce social transfers in order to curb public spending and eventually balance the budget. The florint has become the 'hard currency' in the region, and has made the Hungarian market-place attractive for small entrepreneurs, while its quasi-convertibility has attracted foreign investors, causing them to buy large parts of certain sectors of the Hungarian economy. The Minister of Finance, Mihaly Kupa, favours a mixed economic system similar to the Austrian model.[76]

Hungary is very preoccupied by the fate of the large Hungarian minorities scattered around Slovakia, Ukraine, Romania and Vojvodina, a legacy from the Austro-Hungarian empire. These neighbouring countries have watched Hungarian foreign policy with suspicion, waiting for Hungarian territorial claims to resurface. Their fears can hardly have been allayed by the claim of the Hungarian Prime Minister, Joszef Antall, when taking office in 1990, to be the leader of all Hungarians wherever they might live. Prime Minister Antall, however, stated that Hungary ought not be involved in a campaign to redraw Europe's borders, but should promote the establishment of universal standards for the protection of ethnic minorities.[77] The government has been eager to show that its purpose is benign and has proposed a law on the rights of ethnic minorities, hoping that this law will become an example also for those countries which host Hungarian minorities. The ethnic minorities within Hungary constitute about 10% of the population, of which the Gypsies are the largest group. Hungary has also made cooperation agreements with neighbouring states, conditional upon their respect of the rights of Hungarian minorities. But, so far, only Ukraine has accepted.[78] The Hungarian authorities watch developments in Romania, Slovakia and Vojvodina attentively, but would certainly prefer that the situation of the Hungarian minorities be settled in the countries in which they live, rather than having to deal with additional flows of refugees.

The other new democracies

As for the other new democracies of eastern Europe, membership ambitions may be real, but eligibility is probably some way off. All will have the opportunity to negotiate trade and cooperation agreements with the EC and in due course Europe Agreements. Timetables are difficult to anticipate, since much depends on the establishment of viable governments and the foundations of a modern economy. In practice, however, we may see three distinct groups emerge. First, the Baltic states may well move along this gradual path quite quickly, provided their economies can be sufficiently decoupled from the Russian. The Balts will have the advantage of supportive Nordic neighbours, more industrialized economies and no question of European credentials. The first step was taken in spring 1992, when cooperation agreements were negotiated between the Baltic states and the Community, and an agreement has been reached concerning balance of payments assistance and support programmes.

The Balkan countries form the second group. Although they have had to wait longer than the Visegrad Three, Bulgaria and Romania are both now close to signing Europe Agreements. Conditions in Bulgaria seem to be more favourable than in Romania in terms of the economic reform process, political stability and the treatment of ethnic minorities. The signals coming out of Romania as regards the process of democratization have not been altogether reassuring. The much delayed presidential election eventually took place on 4 and 11 October, with President Ion Iliescu remaining in office. Although he symbolizes for many Romanians the link with the old regime under Nicolae Ceausescu, his continued popularity underlines the influence of the old communist *nomenklatura*. Romania has a bad record in creating and respecting the rights of ethnic minorities, which has led to a dramatic outflow of ethnic Germans, Hungarians and Gypsies and has exacerbated relations with several other European countries, including Germany.

The position of the remaining Balkan countries is more difficult still. Slovenia and Croatia – Catholic countries with substantial expatriate communities in Germany, as well as close economic and social links with Austria, Germany and Italy – have a potentially privileged position. But the Orthodox and Muslim countries emerging out of Yugoslavia, as well as Albania, might have more difficulties in finding ready support from western countries. The inherent risk is that the remaining Balkan countries may in effect be condemned to a peripheral and 'underclass' status for many years.

The third group consists of the European parts of the CIS. These may well want to follow the route which they believe leads to EC membership. Indeed, in Byelorussia, Moldova and Ukraine, signs of such an emerging preference can already be detected, although they are as yet hardly in a position to handle the requirements of trade and cooperation agreements with the EC. Whether Russians see themselves in this category has become a potentially important issue for the EC as well as for Russian policy.

3.3 South European countries

Turkey

As far back as 1963, the EC conceded to Turkey the principle of eventual eligibility for full membership, the date 1997 was even set in the Ankara agreement of association. The relations between the EC and Turkey were set to develop along lines outlined in the Ankara agreement, but in reality progress has been slow and patchy, and today there is still a long way to go in order to achieve the goal of a customs union in 1995. Periodically, Turkish governments, backed by the military and academic elite, have indicated their intention to pursue the goal of membership. Turkey eventually presented its application in 1987, contrary to warnings from inside the Community that the timing was not right.

In December 1989, the Commission declared in its Opinion that neither Turkey nor the EC, whose first priority was the completion of the internal market, was ready to open enlargement negotiations. The Commission was preoccupied by two general considerations: the size of Turkey and its population (which is expected to grow substantially during the next decades); and the economic and political situation in Turkey. The Commission was not convinced that Turkey would be able to handle the adjustment problems of an accession, were it to become member of the EC. The democratic institutions of Turkey were judged to be insufficiently developed and there were important problems in the field of human rights. The dispute over Cyprus with a Community member state was deemed to have a 'negative effect' on the assessment of the political situation in Turkey. The Commission pointed out that difficulties would arise in the EC budget as regards the CAP and the structural funds, since the level of economic development in Turkey did not reach the Community average. The Commission also noted that free access of Turkish labour to the Community would give rise to fears in the member states, especially if they were undergoing a period of high unemployment. It therefore argued that Turkey was 'not yet ready', a position which the Council endorsed on 20 December 1989. The immediate reaction of the Turkish government was disappointment, but as the Commission did not deny Turkey's eligibility to become member, the politicians stated they were ready to pursue the application at a later stage.[79]

In 1996, Turkey's association agreement with the Community will come to an end. Turkish policy has remained set on EC membership, although changes in its immediate political environment may gradually cause other poles of foreign policy to carry more appeal. Recently, the Turkish government is said to have become more realistic about the chances and timing of EC membership.[80] In June 1992, the European Parliament's Committee for Foreign Affairs and Security adopted the Dury report on EC/Turkish relations. The report confirms the change in Turkish attitudes towards membership: 'Membership has not been forgotten but no longer seems to be a government obsession.'[81] The report continues: 'Relations with Europe have to be improved; Turkey may one day be part of Europe, but its main intention is to play a regional role which will be of prime importance.' Finally, the report notes that although progress has been made in the democratization process and the field of human rights, many problems remain to be solved.

The change in attitude towards the EC is in part due to Turkey's new enhanced role in central Asia and southeast Europe, brought about by the break-up of the Soviet Union and the civil war in Yugoslavia. The Turks have found a new dimension in their foreign policy in that the central Asian republics of the CIS and the Muslim communities of Bulgaria and Bosnia-Herzegovina look upon Turkey for political and economic assistance. In these areas there are Turkish minorities that all suffered under communist regimes, or still live under the threat of civil war. For them, Turkey has come to stand out as a guarantor of stability.[82] The central Asian republics (Azerbaijan, Turkmenistan, Uzbekistan, Kyrgyzstan, Kazakhstan and Tajikistan) in particular have placed their hopes in Turkey. They speak Turkic languages and share a common cultural and religious tradition with Turkey. On the Turkish side, this development has been viewed with both enthusiasm and apprehension. Turkey has offered a wide range of technical and cultural programmes, but the task of modernization is enormous and the Turks want support from elsewhere, notably the EC. The EC's new policy towards Turkey is to encourage Turkey to take on the challenge of its role in central Asia, but so far this has not been translated into monetary terms. It has been suggested that this new role could be compared with the position of the reunified Germany, which receives pleas for assistance from CEE countries.[83]

From this new situation follows an argument that the Community should not simply turn away the Turkish membership application, since Turkey has such a crucial role to play as a stabilizing power in this historically troubled region. Secular Turkey could also set a precedent for fundamentalist Muslim countries in terms of integration with the western world and could therefore strengthen Turkey's role against fundamentalist tendencies. The conclusions of the European Council in Lisbon in June 1992 confirmed that 'the

Turkish role in the present European political situation is of the greatest importance and that there is every reason to intensify cooperation and develop relations with Turkey in line with the prospect laid down in the Association Agreement of 1964 including a political dialogue at the highest level'.[84]

Similarly, a report on closer relations between the EC and Turkey, presented by the British as the incoming presidency in June 1992, reconfirmed the 'significant role' Turkey played as a regional power in the proximity of three regions of increasing instability and highlighted the fact that Turkey is a member of NATO, an applicant for EC membership and probably a future associate member of WEU. Therefore, the report argued, the Twelve 'have an interest in establishing relations with Turkey which reflect and take advantage of these unique and particular factors and in giving consideration to Turkey in their debate on European construction'.[85] The EC foreign ministers agreed on the necessity to create closer political and economic links with Ankara, but several member states found that the report did not place sufficient emphasis on Turkish violations of human rights.[86]

Despite well-intentioned moves to prepare the ground for closer cooperation, the Turkish case will continue to provoke great controversy within the EC because it raises such wide-ranging issues, complicated by the strained relationship with Greece and the questioning of its European identity by many in the EC. During the first half of 1992, there was a sharpening of German policy towards Turkey. This came to the forefront in spring 1992 when hard words were exchanged between the German Foreign Minister, Hans-Dietrich Genscher, and the Turkish President, Turgut Ozal, over the use of German arms in the Turkish army's attacks on Kurdish settlements. The affair led to a ban on German arms sales to Turkey (a NATO ally). It also had serious domestic political implications in Germany, forcing the Minister of Defence, Gerhard Stoltenberg, to resign. Relations soured to the point at which Chancellor Kohl rejected President Bush's appeal for Turkish membership of the EC, calling the Turkish actions against the Kurds a 'total contravention' of the Helsinki Final Act.[87] Klaus

Kinkel followed the line of his predecessor when he pointed out in July 1992 that Turkey's accession would pose a serious problem because of the flow of migrant workers into Germany. He confirmed, however, that Germany would make every effort to bring Turkey closer to the Community, even to assist in its aspiration to become a member, but only on certain conditions, in particular full respect of human rights.[88]

There were also diplomatic forays by the British and the French to Ankara in the pursuit of warmer relations. The French President, François Mitterrand, visited Turkey in April 1992, promising that the EC would shortly look into the Turkish application for membership, and that France had no objections in principle to this.[89] The French visit was followed by a visit from the British Foreign Secretary, Douglas Hurd. He reassured the Turkish government of UK support for a new role for Turkey in Europe which 'goes beyond Turkey's membership of NATO'.[90] In this context, it should be noted that Turkey was offered the chance to become an associate member of the WEU at the Maastricht European Council.

The most probable short-term outlook is that the membership application will remain blocked, but that there will be increasing pressures within the EC to improve or redesign the association agreement. This will not be achievable, however, unless the Greek blockage can be overcome either from Athens or by the 11 EC members finding a way of overruling the Greeks. Meanwhile, the Turks hope that, with efforts on all sides, the customs union with the EC will be completed in 1996. They are also waiting for the EC to reactivate the association agreement's fourth financial protocol, providing Turkey with substantial financial aid.[91] An important agreement was reached in the summer of 1992, when Greece finally lifted its blockage of Turkish access to the financial provisions of the revised policy towards Mediterranean countries. This was facilitated by the Council's statement on Cyprus, which supports the unity, independence, sovereignty and territorial integrity of the island.[92]

Malta[93]

Malta and Cyprus both handed in their EC membership applications in summer 1990. The Commission is at work on its Opinion on the two applications. The Conclusions of the European Council in Lisbon in June 1992 stated that 'Relations with Cyprus and Malta will be developed and strengthened by building on the association agreements and by developing the political dialogue'. The European Council has deferred to a later date the accession of both countries, while hoping that a continued progress towards closer cooperation with the Community will have a positive impact on their internal political and economic development.

Malta signed its first association agreement with the EC in 1970, which was subsequently extended by a second and then a third (which runs to October 1993). The association with the Community foresees the gradual establishment of a customs union, and, although Malta has benefited from increased trade with the EC, economic relations between the two have never come close to this objective. The turning-point in Maltese politics came in 1987, when a Labour government had to hand over the governing position to the Nationalist Party. This party describes itself as ideologically close to the Christian Democratic parties in the EC member states. The Labour Party position was weakened already in 1984, when the party changed leadership from the controversial pro-Libyan Dominic Mintoff to the more moderate Carmelo Mifsud Bonnici. The political atmosphere during the 1970s and early 1980s was characterized by violent clashes between the supporters of the two main parties and a subsequent political polarization of society. The Nationalist Party won the general election in 1987 on a programme of change which promised a reorientation of the economic and political principles of Maltese politics. Its leader, Edward Fenech Adami, promised a sweeping reorganization of the large state-owned industrial sector through the establishment of Malta as a financial centre, competing with, say, Luxembourg, Jersey and Monte Carlo, and attracting foreign investment in the high-technology industry by granting tax-relief schemes and improving infrastructure. A second feature of the Nationalist Party's reforms was a general rapprochement to the EC, which eventually led to the decision to present Malta's application for membership.

Malta applied for membership of the Community in July 1990, only a week after Cyprus. Very strong criticism has come from the Labour Party, which argues that the current association agreement remains the best policy. Some economists and industrial leaders fear that the competitive pressures inside the EC would damage Maltese industry, which has traditionally been protected by restrictions on foreign investment and imports.

The Maltese application has provoked some concern in the EC. One striking reaction has been the insistence on the institutional complications of a 'micro-state' as a member. Fears have been expressed that this might dilute the effectiveness of the EC. Malta has, moreover, been pressed to redefine its close ties with the Libyan government (which have been loosened, but not abandoned), and many commentators consider its status of non-alignment a problem. Both features of Maltese foreign policy could be difficult to reconcile with the *acquis communautaire* and *politique* of the EC. In the economic field, the government's endeavours to open up the Maltese economy have been welcomed in the EC, but fall short of what would be required by the internal market. The experience of the Maltese association agreement suggests that an economic integration would need substantial additional efforts.

On the other hand, a factor that favours early Maltese accession to the Community is the small size of the country's economy and population (350,000 people), in that the scale of adjustment for the EC is limited. Malta's agricultural and fishing sector is quite small (4% of GNP in 1989),[94] while a large part of national income originates from tourism. It has also a good track record in low unemployment (4.1% in 1990),[95] low inflation (3.5% in 1991) and a per capita income of $6,371; the EC average in 1990 was $15,300,[96] when Greece and Portugal had lower per capita income than Malta. Malta trades extensively with the EC (75% of total trade in 1990), with Italy, Germany and the United Kingdom providing the largest share of Maltese imports.

In the general election of February 1992, the ruling Nationalist

Party confirmed its position by increasing its majority in parliament. The election campaign had brought out EC policy as a key issue; in winning its majority, the government considers it has a strong mandate for its pro-EC policy. Prime Minister Fenech Adami pronounced his intention vigorously to pursue the Maltese membership application.[97] The government hopes to get support from the southern EC member states to make sure that the country's application will be considered at the same time as those of the EFTA candidates.

Cyprus

Cyprus applied for membership in summer 1990, a week before Malta. Although there are obvious similarities between the two states – as two island communities in the Mediterranean – the political challenge that Cyprus poses to the EC is quite different.

Cyprus negotiated an association agreement with the Community in 1972.[98] Further progress with the agreement was interrupted in 1974 by the Turkish invasion of the island. The EC response was to freeze its development until the dispute was resolved, insisting that the trade and other provisions of the agreement should apply to the whole island. Only in 1987 did the EC sign a protocol which sets out the conditions for the second stage of the agreement and paves the way for the establishment of a customs union, to be achieved in stages over a ten-year period.

The role of the EC in the dispute between Greece and Turkey over the governance of Cyprus became more delicate when Greece joined the Community in 1981 and tried to use the EC framework to endorse its policy towards Turkey, including the Cyprus issue. In principle, EC member states and EC institutions have been reluctant to take sides in the disputes of other members when these are considered internal or bilateral (e.g. Northern Ireland, Gibraltar, the Basque countries). But in the case of Cyprus this has been very difficult to achieve and has greatly complicated the Community's relationship with Turkey. The Greek government persuaded the European Council, in Rhodes 1988 and in Dublin 1990, to issue statements noting that its relations with Turkey were 'affected' by the Cyprus problem. The European Parliament took an even harder line in a resolution adopted in May 1988. This noted that 'the unlawful occupation of part of the territory of a country associated to the Community (i.e. Cyprus) by the military forces of another country, also associated with the Community (i.e. Turkey), presents a major stumbling block to the normalization of relations with the latter, viz. Turkey'.[99]

The eventual membership of the EC of both Cyprus and Turkey has become linked with the need for a settlement between the Turkish and Greek Cypriots. The EC/Cyprus joint parliamentary committee issued on 17 July 1992 a statement urging the Commission to produce a positive Opinion on Cyprus's application for membership. The parliamentarians noted in the resolution that the Lisbon summit's Conclusions did not seem to meet the aspirations of the Cypriots.[100]

The Greek Cypriot government's decision to seek membership of the EC was undoubtedly influenced by the uncompromising position of the Turkish Cypriot leader, Rauf Denktash, in the UN peace talks in 1988, which ended with the Turkish Cypriot side leaving the negotiation table. The Greek Cypriot President, George Vassiliou, stated in July 1990 that he hoped the Turkish Cypriot leadership would also take part in the negotiations with the Community, and that the prospect of membership could help in achieving an agreement to reunite the island.[101] The response of the Turkish Cypriots, who had not been consulted before the move, was cold, close to hostile, with diplomatic contacts broken off for several months.[102] EC member states reacted without enthusiasm to the Cypriot application, but tried under the Luxembourg presidency in 1991 to launch an initiative for mediation between the two communities – so far without success.

During the summer of 1992 a new attempt was made to solve the deadlock over the island. The compromise elaborated by the UN and promoted by its Secretary-General, Boutros Boutros-Ghali, was based on the introduction of a federal system of government. Exploratory talks came to a standstill when the Turkish Cypriot side rejected a plan that aimed at redrawing the borders of the communities. Turkish Cypriots constitute 18% of the population and at present occupy 37% of the territory. The plan proposed that they accept 28% of the territory, but Rauf Denktash has insisted on 30%. The difference of 2% may not seem much, but the area includes the important region of Morfou, which, according to Denktash, is not negotiable. This region generates 40% of Turkish Cypriot foreign earnings.[103]

The Greek Cypriot economy has made remarkable progress, mainly in the tourist and agricultural sectors, and Cyprus has also become an offshore financial centre. In 1990, 53% of imports originated in the EC, while 47% of exports went to EC member states, mainly Greece and Britain.[104] The per capita income of the Greek Cypriots is three times higher than that of the Turkish Cypriots, close to that of Spain. The Turkish part is dependent on financial support and investments from Ankara, and 50,000 Turks were settled on the island to take over the farms which Greek Cypriots had been forced to abandon. The Greek Cypriot government argues that the Turkish community's economy could be brought up to the level of the Greek within two years of reunification.

4

What can be learnt from past experiences?

The Community has only recently completed negotiations with two groups of countries, namely the EFTA states and Poland, Hungary and the CSFR. These exercises have led to the creation of the EEA and the signing of the Europe Agreements. Although the conditions and starting points of the negotiations were very different, they provide good examples for analysing where the hurdles lie when forging new forms of cooperation between the EC and other countries. The origins of the negotiations stem from similar sets of preoccupations. Both the EFTA states and the newly established market economies in the east were eager to forge links with an increasingly dynamic Community, and, in particular, to gain access to the internal market.

4.1 The European Economic Area
The EFTA states have for a long time been unilaterally adapting to EC regulations, an unsatisfactory situation for deep-rooted parliamentary democracies. The EC, conversely, sought to head off membership applications until, at least, the accomplishment of the internal market in 1993. In contrast with the strategy of the 1970s, the Community was at the end of the 1980s prepared to look for alternative or 'third-way' solutions. The exercise has, however, thus far been frustrating for both parties and the outcome so short of what was desired that several of the countries have tabled membership applications or have announced their intention to do so.

The relationship between the EC and EFTA was established already in the early days of the European integration process. The different objectives and institutional structures of EFTA and the Community reflected very different views on how far countries were prepared to go down the road of supranational integration. The EFTA states favoured free trade and intergovernmental cooperation, but feared the loss of sovereignty and the transfer of power to independent institutions. They created an organization which would look after their commercial interests and supply them with a coherent framework to facilitate contacts with the Community. At the time of the first enlargement of the EC, the links with the remaining EFTA countries were codified in bilateral free trade agreements. Until the launch of the Luxembourg process in 1984, which marked the starting-point for intensified cooperation, relations between the EC and EFTA could be characterized as stable and uneventful. However, in the mid-1980s, the renewed dynamics of the EC found the existing cooperation framework unable to adapt to rapid change; industrialists in the EFTA countries became increasingly worried about the effects on their competitive position. The patchy and pragmatic approach of the Luxembourg process culminated in 1989 when President Delors, in a speech to the European Parliament, opened the door for a new kind of partnership with the EFTA countries.[1]

The negotiations launched between the EFTA countries and the EC with a view to setting up the EEA were envisaged as an easy and expedient exercise. But, after the opening of the formal negotiations in June 1990, frustrations increased on both sides. At long last, the EEA was signed in Portugal on 2 May 1992, although it remains to be seen whether ratification of the Treaty will be completed before the end of 1992 to enter into force in 1993.[2] It is important to analyse why the negotiations have been so difficult between partners that know each other well from many years of fruitful cooperation and that share the same basic economic, social and political systems.

A set of asymmetries has emerged during the negotiations.[3] First, the EEA is not equally important to all the participants. The

EFTA countries saw in President Delors's offer of a new institutionalized approach to the EC/EFTA relationship a solution to their internal dilemma concerning European integration and their fear of becoming economically isolated from the dynamic developments in the Community. The EEA would give them access to the four freedoms of the internal market and the flanking policies without having to deal with the difficult question of EC membership. The internal situation of several EFTA states was such that governments preferred to defer discussions on issues related to EC membership: neutrality, loss of sovereignty, sharing of resources, restructuring of the agricultural sector and constitutional changes.

The Community was busy implementing the internal market programme and testing out the new decision-making procedures and institutional provisions laid down in the Single European Act. The EC had only just digested the southern enlargement and resolved its old structural and budgetary problems through the Delors-1 package. It was determined not to lose its newly recovered dynamics or to risk becoming bogged down in tiresome and time-consuming membership negotiations. The proposal made by President Delors is often interpreted as a pre-emptive strike to prevent the EFTA countries from presenting their membership applications. The EFTA countries have always been considered important partners, but, unlike them, the Community's market power made it less dependent on formally enlarging the single market. Because the EFTA countries are regarded as unproblematic, well-off and sympathetic, the EC has tended to concentrate its political energies on other areas in Europe, where the developments were more dramatic and less predictable.

Second, the preferences of the EFTA governments on what the EEA should offer in terms of institutional and legal framework did not correspond to what the Community was either able or willing to deliver. At the outset of the negotiations, the EC stipulated some basic principles which the EFTA states accepted: the negotiations should be based on the relevant *acquis communautaire* defined jointly; there should be real reciprocity between the parties, meaning that the EFTA countries should contribute (financially) towards cohesion within the Community; both parties' decision-making processes should remain independent and intact; and the EFTA governments should negotiate as a group.

Third, the objectives of members of the EFTA group concerning integration with the Community were diverging from the outset (Austria's membership application in mid-1989) and became increasingly so (Sweden's membership application mid-1991). Following on from these different objectives about the goal of closer integration were different ideas about what the EEA should offer in terms of real decision-making power and whether the EEA was a long- or short-term alternative to membership.

The scope of the agreement – the four freedoms and the flanking policies – did not pose any insurmountable problems. The most contentious areas, Norwegian and Icelandic fishing resources in exchange for access to EC markets and conditions for road transport through Switzerland and Austria, were either partly solved within the scope of the agreement or dealt with on a bilateral basis. The list of derogations that the EFTA governments initially presented was reduced by the EC to a minimum and resolved through transitional measures – the traditional Community way of dealing with adaptation to the *acquis communautaire*. An agreement was found on financial support to the poorer EC countries, Spain, Portugal, Greece and Ireland, after tough negotiations.

The real stumbling block has been the institutional and legal dimension of the EEA. The two-pillar structure, with decision-making to occur through 'osmosis', as proposed by Jacques Delors, is to be made operational through participation by the EFTA countries in a network of working groups and committees. EFTA will set up an agency to mirror the Commission, responsible for the implementation and surveillance of the agreement in the field of competition, and a joint committee of high-level civil servants will ensure continued contact between the parties throughout the decision-making process. This arrangement falls well short of the 'genuine participation in decisions in substance and in form'[4] that the EFTA countries had set out to achieve. Arguably, they might have expected too much when asking for real participation in the decision-making process. It is, after all, only full membership that gives access to the rights and obligations of the Community framework, and the EC feels it necessary to ensure that the distinction between membership and non-membership does not deteriorate.

The dilemma of how to find solutions acceptable to the EFTA countries, while at the same time respecting the Community's internal structure and *acquis communautaire*, was vividly revealed in the controversy over the EEA Court. This has raised an important question of principle, where the legal homogeneity of the EEA has been argued to be at odds with the special role given to the ECJ by the Community treaties. The formula proposed was an EEA Court, where judges from the ECJ and from EFTA would share jurisdiction over the EEA and together interpret the provisions of the EEA treaty and future legislation. But the ECJ ruled on 14 December 1991 that the competences given to the EEA Court were incompatible with the EC treaties, in so far as the interpretation of EEA legislation might not conform with the interpretation of the EC legislation, since the objectives of the EC and the EEA are in crucial respects different. The EEA Court, it was argued, could become a threat to the Community legal order and thereby endanger the foundations of the EC.[5] The position of the ECJ was supported by the European Parliament, which plays a crucial role in the ratification process of the EEA by its power of veto. The European Parliament demanded that an amended EEA treaty should be submitted again to the Court for opinion. In return, the Court gave the European Parliament the right to present its observations on the treaty, a right which the Parliament does not normally have.

The Community respected the judgment of the Court and had to accept, as did the EFTA states, that the contracting parties must alter the judicial system proposed for the EEA in order to keep the Community's autonomy intact. The Commission and the EFTA countries have found a political compromise, and the ECJ has now endorsed the revised treaty. The joint committee has come to play an enhanced role. Article 105.2 of the treaty states that:

The EEA Joint Committee shall keep under constant review the development of the case law of the Court of Justice of the European Communities and the EFTA Court. To this end judgments of these Courts shall be transmitted to the EEA Joint Committee which shall act so as to preserve the homogeneous interpretation of the Agreement.[6]

If the Joint Committee, which is composed of high civil servants of the contracting parties, cannot find agreement on homogeneous interpretation of case law brought in front of it, the agreement gives the parties the possibility to request the ECJ to rule on the interpretation. If the parties cannot settle the dispute, they can either take safeguard measures or suspend parts of the agreement.

This compromise rests on a formula for arbitration which cannot give a 100% guarantee of legal homogeneity within the EEA. The EFTA states have accepted a solution which is not fully satisfactory in terms of democratic accountability. This perhaps matters less, in that it is widely believed that the EEA agreement may not be long-lived, as so many EFTA countries are expected to join the EC in the future.[7] The dispute over the provisions of the EEA agreement with the ECJ really brought home to the EFTA states that full membership was the only road to influencing the content and interpretation of Community law.

Lessons can be drawn from the EEA exercise on the difficulties of creating viable alternatives to an EC membership. The building of a 'half-way house' confronts the negotiators with more problems than a straightforward membership negotiation. The latter does not put the *acquis communautaire* in question or require novel legal arrangements, but accepts the limits of scope of the negotiations and focuses subsequently on the terms of entry. For the Community, economic integration is inextricably linked to political integration. To separate the two, as the EEA concept did, contradicts the basic principles and practices of the Community.

The EEA has often been cited as a possible antechamber for other potential membership candidates. In its present form, it does not seem a viable option. The idea behind the creation of the EEA

135

originated from a long-standing cooperation between two groups of countries with similar economic and social characteristics and with societies which were founded on the same set of values and principles. The EEA in itself puts high demands on political and administrative skills, as well as requiring tight coordination among the EFTA states to speak with one voice in the consultation procedure with the Commission and surveillance mechanisms. The EEA is built on the assumption that the contracting parties share the similar level of economic development with sophisticated economic structures and markets. In addition, it does not imply any engagement in foreign and security policies. The EEA cannot therefore be attractive for the CEE countries, which would at present have problems meeting the economic conditions of membership, but would welcome the stability of the foreign and security framework of the Community.

4.2 The Europe Agreements

In December 1991, in the wake of the Maastricht summit, Hungary, the CSFR and Poland signed far-reaching association agreements, the Europe Agreements, with the Community. It had been decided, at the 1990 European Council in Dublin, to create a new type of association agreement with individual CEE countries as a part of the new pattern of relationships in Europe.

The Europe Agreements are 'second-generation' agreements intended to supersede those on trade and cooperation signed with several CEE countries and the EC in 1988 and 1989. They are new instruments aiming at associating the newly established democracies with the European integration process on the basis of gradual implementation of the four freedoms of movement of the EC and the internal market. The Europe Agreements combine an asymmetrical opening of EC markets, technical and economic cooperation and approximation of law with a framework of political dialogue. The agreements are designed to meet the requirements of each individual country and to take into account democratic and economic progress, thus providing scope for a gradual development of the association.

The evolutionary character of the Europe Agreements would then assist Hungary, the CSFR and Poland, and other CEE countries in due course, on their way towards membership of the EC. But the agreements do not give guarantees on this objective, nor do they state the conditions to be fulfilled before negotiations can be envisaged. They facilitate, however, the integration of the economies of these countries with the EC by aligning them to the legal framework of the Community and gradually adapting them to future legislation. The Europe Agreements also promote the strengthening of democratic principles by conditioning future integration with the EC on the development of social and political structures. The Community's objective is to help the countries to sustain the difficult process of economic reform as pressures build up to ease the burden of their societies.

The negotiation of the Europe Agreements was difficult, and the outcome has been criticized by both the recipient countries and many commentators in the EC member states. Criticism is focused primarily on the argument that the Europe Agreements fall short of delivering to the CEE countries the means necessary to succeed in creating well-functioning market economies and stable democracies.[8] The liberalization of trade is designed in practice to permit free flow of industrial goods from the associates to EC markets within a period of five years, while goods from the Community will be granted free access after five to ten years. However, this well-intentioned principle of freedom of goods does not include trade in products which are among the most vital for the CEE countries and the most sensitive for the EC member states: steel, iron, coal, textile and agricultural products. Tariffs and quantitative restrictions will remain on these sensitive products for a period of up to ten years, varying in extent and length for each product group. The Commission resisted demands from some member countries to impose voluntary export restraints, but had to satisfy the fears of the domestic interest groups concerned by subjecting steel, iron, coal and textile to restrictive anti-dumping and safeguard clauses. To what extent these measures will be invoked against producers in Hungary, the CSFR and Poland cannot be predicted, though the position is an improvement on their previous state-trading status. The burden of evidence will lie with the accusing partner, giving the Commission the role of judging the seriousness of each individual case.

Free trade in agricultural products evoked strong protests from many EC farmers, most vocally the French, who urged their governments to take a restrictive position at the negotiation table. Their reactions were out of all proportion to the likely level of CEE exports to EC members. After Polish threats of leaving the table, along with criticism from other member states, the French were persuaded to give in on some of their demands. A deal was struck on the basis of stricter import controls, the right to invoke safeguard measures, were it deemed necessary by France, and a diversion of trade to the former Soviet Union through a condition to buy food for the CIS states from the CEE countries using an emergency loan granted by the EC. Hungary, the CSFR and Poland were far from satisfied with this part of the Europe Agreements, mainly because the sectors hardest hit by restrictive measures are those where the countries best stand a chance to compete successfully in EC markets. These sectors have suffered hard from the breakdown of CMEA trade, and, additionally, the agricultural sector is producing, unable to sell its full production at home, a surplus as a result of the lifting of subsidized prices on food.

Freedom of labour movement is far from being resolved in the Europe Agreements because of fears in the EC countries (most of all Germany) of a poverty-driven mass migration. It is difficult to foresee how this sensitive issue will develop in the framework of the Europe Agreements, but there seems to be a consensus among EC political leaders that full freedom of movement cannot be granted until the economic situation in the countries is such that it excludes this kind of migration. So far the Europe Agreements give recognition to those workers who are lawfully employed in EC member states, a provision which make workers from the east subject to restrictive national laws on employment of foreigners. Whether this arrangement will prove durable remains to be seen.

The Europe Agreements also open a political dialogue which is intended to familiarize the CEE countries with the political framework and foreign policy activities of the Community. The structures have not yet been worked out as a fully-fledged process of political consultation, but in principle the framework is flexible enough to develop into a more extensive cooperation if the partners so wish. Hungary, the CSFR and Poland were disappointed that the agreements did no more than acknowledge their objective of future membership of the EC. The EC member states did not want to sign up for either a timetable or conditions for accession, maybe in order not to repeat mistakes of the past in giving promises which have proved difficult to honour. The wording of the compromise takes note of the wish of the three countries to become members of the Community in the future.

Opinions diverge on how far the Europe Agreements will supply the support necessary to ensure political stability and economic development. Those who support the agreements argue that the Community responded fast to unprecedented problems, and, given the pressures from vested interests within the EC, they managed to claim that the Europe Agreements have ensured the best deal for the three countries at this stage. They underline the flexibility and evolutionary character of the agreements, which makes a gradual deepening of the cooperation possible, as soon as the associates are ready. They take a prudent approach on the question of future membership of the EC, arguing that the CEE countries need time to prepare not only their economies but also their populations for the requirements of EC membership. Enlargement should be a gradual and pragmatic process, in which developments in the candidate countries will show if, when and how they can accede the Community.

Those who are critical of the Europe Agreements argue that, even though the agreements are definitely a step in the right direction, they fail to give Hungary, the CSFR and Poland a substantive and unambiguous framework within which to build up their new democracies. The criticism falls in two categories: economic and political. In the economic area, the Europe Agreements do not fully extend the four freedoms of the internal market to the three countries, but limit free trade on the products most suitable for export, especially as regards agricultural products. In the political field, they do not constitute a comprehensive strategy for the future of European integration, and the place of Hungary, the CSFR and Poland within it. The critics had wanted a clearer signal to these countries on a strategy towards future enlargements, maybe a promise of considering EC membership at the stage when the three countries fulfil specific basic requirements. A clearer strategy on the future of Europe would enable the CEE countries, according to commentators, both to deal with their internal reform process and to create frameworks of cooperation among themselves.

The Community envisages extending a framework of cooperation to other states in eastern Europe. The cooperation will be based on Europe Agreements, to be negotiated as soon as possible with Bulgaria and Romania, and trade and cooperation agreements with the Baltic States, Albania, Slovenia and possibly Croatia, with Europe Agreements to follow in due course. Future developments will show whether it will be possible to extend the network also to other break-away republics of Yugoslavia and to some of the republics of CIS. But the EC will have to think hard about whether to restrict Europe Agreements to those countries that it is prepared, in principle, to envisage as possible future members.

In parallel to the Community's endeavour, regional groups are being created, such as the Central European Initiative in south-eastern Europe and the revival of the old Hanseatic League among the countries around the Baltic Sea and Norway. Regional cooperation frameworks may well have an important role to play in creating an integrated and all-embracing European structure. In time they may have to be taken more actively into account by the EC.[9]

Notes

Chapter 2

1 Commission of the European Communities, *Briefing Note, Background Report*, ISEC/B33/91, 18 December 1991.

2 European Council, *Presidency Conclusions*, Maastricht, 9 and 10 December 1991.

3 Five-Institute Report, *The European Community: Progress or Decline?*, RIIA, London, 1983, pp. 41–2.

4 *Europe*, 20/21 July 1992, No. 5776.

5 WEU Ministerial Council, 19 June in Petersberg (Bonn), *Europe Documents*, 23 June 1992, No. 1787.

6 Dr Willem van Eekelen, in a speech given at Chatham House, 22 September 1992.

7 An analysis of the concept of subsidiarity can be found in Marc Wilke and Helen Wallace, *Subsidiarity: Approaches to Power-sharing in the European Community*, RIIA Discussion Paper No. 27, RIIA, London, 1990.

8 President Delors, quoted in *Europe*, 25 June 1992, No. 5757.

9 President Delors, quoted in *Europe*, Special Edition, European Council in Lisbon, 28 June 1992.

10 In 1990, EFTA GNP was 668.2 becus, while EC GNP was 6440.0 becus. Information in Eurostat/EFTA, *Facts through figures. A statistical portrait of EFTA in the European Economic Area*, Statistical Office of the EC, Luxembourg, 1992.

11 The Treaty of Rome, Articles 117–22, enumerates certain areas in social policy regarding conditions for workers where the EC could take action. When the Council of Ministers legislates under these articles, unanimity is required. Article 100a, on the other hand,

stipulates that measures for the protection of workers' health are to be adopted by qualified majority.

12 For a discussion of various concepts used in the context of the widening of the EC, see Helen Wallace, *Europe: The Challenge of Diversity*, Chatham House Paper No. 29, RIIA, London, 1985. See also Michael Mertes and Norbert J. Prill, 'Europäische Strukturen: Ein Plädoyer für institutionelle Ökonomie', *Europa Archiv*, No. 6, 25 March 1992. (An English-language version of this article appears in *International Affairs*, Vol. 67, No. 4, 1992.)

13 This chapter is partly based on information and impressions collected during a visit to Brussels in March 1992. The author met civil servants at permanent representations of the EC member states and EFTA countries, the Commission and the EFTA secretariat.

14 'The Community's Enlargement: The Benelux Memorandum', submitted to the European Council of Lisbon, *Europe Documents*, 27 June 1992, No. 1789.

15 Ibid.

16 *Europe*, 20/21 July 1992, No. 5776.

17 See, for instance, an interview with Elisabeth Guigou, 'Les Européens et leur destin', *Politique Internationale*, No. 51, 1991. President Mitterrand at the Lisbon European Council repeated his thinking along the lines of a confederal structure, especially in order to integrate central and east European counties, *Europe*, 27 June 1992, No. 5759, p. 4.

18 *Europe*, 11 September 1992, No. 5813.

19 The Portuguese Foreign Minister, Joao de Pinheiro, quoted in *Europe*, 22/23 June 1992, No. 5755, p. 3.

20 Article J.4.4 reads: 'The policy of the Union in accordance with this Article shall not prejudice the specific character of the security and defence policy of certain Member States...'.

21 Frans Andriessen, in a speech at the UK Presidency Conference, 'Europe and the World after 1992', London, 7 September 1992.

22 European Commission, 'Opinion on Greek application for membership', *Bulletin of the European Communities*, supplement 2/76, 29 January 1976.

23 Commission of the European Communities, *Commission Opinion on Turkey's Request for Accession to the Community*, SEC(89) 2290 final, Brussels, 20 December 1989.

24 *The Times*, 'Leaders urged to unify Europe', 27 June 1992.
25 *Europe*, No. 5727, 11/12 May 1992. No premature deductions should have been drawn from the press coverage of either Delors's apparent position or the overall position of the Commission. Some commentators had been reading too much into isolated comments, and the report to Lisbon should be read carefully. Commissioners are well aware of the sensitivity of the institutional issues, especially during the ratification process of the Maastricht agreement.
26 See comments in *The Guardian*, 1 May 1992, 'Delors plans radical revamp for EC top body'; *The Sunday Telegraph*, 3 May 1992, 'Delors plan to rule Europe'; *The Financial Times*, 2/3 May 1992, 'EEA treaty to spur hot debate on bigger EC', and 5 May 1992, 'All at sea in Europe'.
27 Jacques Delors in *Europe*, 4/5 May 1992.
28 Frans Andriessen, *Towards a Community of Twenty-Four?*, 69th Plenary Assembly of Eurochambers, Economic and Social Committee, Brussels, 19 April 1991.
29 European Parliament, *Report on the Community Enlargement and Relations with Other European Countries*, DOC-EN/RR/10695, 26 March 1991.
30 The European Parliament's Resolution on the results of the Intergovernmental Conferences, Resolution A3-0123/92, published in *Europe Documents*, 10 April 1992, No. 1769.
31 *Europe*, 27 June 1992, No. 5759.
32 Quoted in 'Memorandum by Gary Titley, MEP', House of Lords Select Committee on the European Communities, *Enlargement of the Community – Minutes of Evidence*', London, HMSO, 12 March 1992.
33 Hans-Gert Pöttering, *Europe*, 25 April 1992.
34 'Memorandum by Edward McMillan-Scott', House of Lords Select Committee on the European Communities, *Enlargement of the Community – Minutes of Evidence*, London, HMSO, 12 March 1992.
35 *The Financial Times*, 'EC vows to ratify Maastricht', 4 June 1992.
36 Joint statement by M. François Mitterrand, President of the French Republic, and Dr Helmut Kohl, Chancellor of the Federal Republic of Germany (Paris, 3 June 1992), Speeches and statements, French Embassy in London, 3 June 1992.

37 *The Financial Times*, 'British premier pledges steps to decentralise EC', 4 June 1992.
38 *The Financial Times*, 'Partners leave Danes to ponder their fate', 5 June 1992.
39 Quoted in *Europe*, 19 June 1992, No. 5753, p. 5.
40 *The Guardian*, 'Danes and a Demon', 21 August 1992.
41 *Europe*, 28/29 September 1992, No. 5824.
42 *Europe*, 21 August 1992, No. 5798, and 23 September 1992, No. 5820.
43 *Le Monde*, 'Un sondage de l'IFPO confirme la progression du "non"', 5 August 1992.
44 *Libération*, 'Le référendum, une mise à l'épreuve pour les parties', 31 August 1992.
45 From the French, 'l'enjeu Mitterrand'.
46 *Le Monde*, 'Pièges d'une victoire', 22 September 1992.
47 *Le Monde*, op cit.
48 *Europe*, 3 July 1992, No. 5765.
49 *Europe*, 25 June 1992, No. 5757.
50 John Major, in a speech given at the UK Presidency Conference, 'Europe and the World after 1992', London, 7 September 1992.

Chapter 3

1 Paul Luif, 'Austria', in Helen Wallace (ed.), *The Wider Western Europe: Reshaping the EC/EFTA Relationship*, Pinter/RIIA, London, 1991.
2 Eurostat/EFTA, *Facts through figures. A statistical portrait of EFTA in the European Economic Area*, Statistical Office of the EC, Luxembourg, 1992.
3 Manfred Scheich, in a speech given at Chatham House, London, 2 February 1990.
4 Alois Mock, 'L'Autriche et l'intégration de l'Europe', *Revue de politique internationale*, No. 936, April 1989.
5 Alois Mock, *Integration and Disintegration in the New Europe*, speech given at Chatham House, London, 3 February 1992; and in 'EC fails – and nearly falls apart', *Austria. Business & Economy*, Vol. 3, No. 8, October 1991.
6 'L'Euroscepticisme gagne l'Autriche', *Le Monde*, 25 February 1992.
7 *The Guardian*, 'Austrian application throws EC members into confusion', 18 July 1989, and *The Financial Times*, 'Belgium throws

a spanner in the works as Austria applies for entry to Community',
18 July 1989.

8   *Avis de la Commission sur la demande d'adhésion de l'Autriche. Avant-propos et Conclusions*, Commission of the European Communities,
Brussels, 5 August 1991.

9   Statement by the Foreign Minister of Austria, Dr Alois Mock, on
the occasion of the signing of the Treaty on European Union on 7
February 1992 (working translation).

10 Quoted in *Europe*, 13/14 July 1992, No. 5771, p. 4.

11 Rüdiger Görner, *Austria's Cultural Contribution to Europe*, paper
given at UACES conference, March 1992.

12 Fessel+GfK nationwide representative survey, 1991.

13 *Europe*, 28/29 September 1992, No. 5824.

14 The passages on Finland, Norway and Sweden are based on
information collected during a study tour in February 1992.
Interviews were conducted with academics, parliamentarians and
practitioners in the Nordic capitals.

15 Esko Aho in *Veckans Affärer*, No. 23, 5 June 1991.

16 Tapani Paavonen, *Finland's Road to Europe. Changes in institutional
frameworks and economic policies*, University of Turku, Political
History, Publications C:33, 1991.

17 Statement by the Bank of Finland, 8 September 1992.

18 *Hufudstadsbladet*, 'Kursen försvagades med över 15 procent', 9
September 1992, and 'EG-förhandlingar trots flytande mark', 11
September 1992.

19 *Arbeiderbladet*, 'EF sur på Finland', 12 September 1992.

20 *Hufudstadsbladet*, 'Snabb truppreträtt från Balticum', and
'Statsministrarna tar över makten', 19 September 1992.

21 *Finland och ett medlemskap i den Europeiska Gemenskapen. Statsrådets
redogörelse till riksdagen om konsekvenserna av ett EG-medlemskap för
Finland*, 9 January 1992.

22 Jarl Köhler, 'The Next Phase of Enlargement', speech given at the
UK Presidency Conference, 'Europe and the World after 1992',
London, 7 September 1992.

23 Paavo Lipponen, in Mats Kockberg (ed.), *Det nya Europa. En bok om
förändringarna i Europa till Ingvar S. Melins 60-års dag*, Oy Fram Ab,
Vasa, 1992.

24 *Hufudstadsbladet*, 11 September 1992 (n. 18).

25 Statement by Prime Minister Esko Aho, 20 September 1992.

26 Jon Baldvin Hannibalsson, 'Iceland in a Changing Europe –
    Isolation or Integration', speech given at a seminar held by the
    European Commission in Reykjavik, 13 March 1992.
27 Gunnar Helgi Kristinsson, 'Iceland', in Wallace (ed.), *The Wider
    Western Europe*.
28 Information gathered during a visit to the Icelandic Delegation to
    the European Community, March 1992.
29 *Europe*, 12 September 1992, No. 5813.
30 Jon Erik Dolvik *et al.*, *Norsk økonomi og europeisk integrasjon*, FAFO-
    rapport, No. 130, 1991.
31 Holding the chairmanship of EFTA, Gro Harlem Brundtland
    responded to President Delors's initiative at an EFTA summit in
    Oslo in March 1989. She had discussed beforehand with Delors the
    possibility of finding an alternative to membership without losing
    access to the EC's internal market.
32 *Norinform*, 12–28 April 1992.
33 *Norinform*, 'Government shake-up' , 8 September 1992.
34 *Arbeiderbladet*, 'Fiskersønn, EF-storm', 12 September 1992.
35 *Norinform*, 'Maverick politician shakes Labour', 8 September
    1992.
36 *Aftenposten*, 'Enslig svale i EF-saken', 20 September 1992.
37 *Europe*, 8 July 1992, No. 5767.
38 *Norinform*, 'Eurosceptics lead the race', 30 June 1992.
39 *Norinform*, 'Norway still an EC applicant', 9 June 1992.
40 *Aftenposten*, 'Brundtland glad for resultatet', 21 September 1992.
41 *Aftenposten*, 'Fr.p.-velgere til Høyre', 19 September 1992.
42 Foreign Affairs Committee, *Riksdagen, 1990/91:UU 8*.
43 This passage is influenced by Carl-Einar Stålvant, 'Sweden and the
    European Community in 1990', contribution to the *CEPS Yearbook*,
    1991.
44 *Dagens Industri*, 'Sanningens minut för kronan', 9 September 1992;
    Svenska Dagbladet, 'Fri Mark skakar Sverige', 9 September 1992;
    Dagens Nyheter, 'Valuta vände åter', 10 September 1992; *Västerviks
    Tidningen*, 'Räntan upp till 500 procent', 17 September 1992; *The
    Financial Times*, 'Sweden unveils rescue package', 21 September
    1992.
45 Pierre Schori, Under-Secretary of State, in a speech held at
    Chatham House, May 1991.
46 Foreign Affairs Committee, *Riksdagen 1991/92*, No. 19.

47 *Svenska Dagbladet,* 'EG-motståndarnas verklighetsbild korrekt', 18 September 1992.
48 *Commission of the European Communities,* SEC(92) final/II, Brussels, 31 July 1992.
49 *Svenska Dagbladet,* 'Svenskt jordbruk passar inte EG', 2 August 1992.
50 *Dagens Nyheter,* 'Glest Norrland imponerar på EG', 9 September 1992.
51 *Svenska Dagbladet,* 'Sverige välkomnas till EG', 1 August 1992.
52 Sven Hirdman,'EG-medlemskap fråga om solidaritet' *Svenska Dagbladet,* 19 September 1992.
53 *Svenska Dagbladet/Europa,* 'Att vara eller inte vara med', 1 September 1992.
54 *The Financial Times,* 'Neighbours feel the chill winds', 20 July 1992.
55 Press Release, *Federal Council Report on Switzerland's Position in the Process of European Integration,* November 1990.
56 Ibid.
57 Communiqué de presse, *Politique d'intégration européenne: Déclaration du Conseil fédéral,* Berne, 10 May 1991.
58 Speech by René Felber, President of the Confederation at the opening of the International Automobile Exhibition, Geneva, 5 March 1992.
59 René Schwok, *Swiss Identity and European Integration,* paper presented at the Eighth International Conference of Europeanists, Chicago, 28 March 1992.
60 Integration Office of the Federal Ministry of Foreign Affairs/ Federal Ministry of Public Economy, fact sheets in *European Integration,* 'Switzerland/EC/EFTA in figures', 16 September 1991.
61 Christian Faessler in a speech at Wilton Park, 19 September 1992.
62 Information from a civil servant of the Swiss Delegation to the EC, Brussels, March 1992.
63 Kaspar Villiger, 'Villiger casse la baraque', interview in *L'Hebdo,* 6 February 1992.
64 Schwok, op cit. (n. 59).
65 *The Financial Times,* 21 May 1992, 'Swiss cultures clash over request to join Community'.
66 *Europe,* 12 September 1992, No. 5813.
67 See Judy Batt, 'Czechoslovakia in Transition – From Federation to Separation', RIIA Discussion Paper, forthcoming 1993.

68 *The Independent*, 'Slovaks seek their own solutions', 3 May 1992.
69 *The Financial Times*, 'Czechoslovak opposition votes down break-up', 1 October 1992.
70 *The Financial Times*, 'Slovaks fear a costly divorce', 3 September 1992.
71 Ibid.
72 *The Independent*, 'Triumph for Walesa as new PM is elected', 6 June 1992.
73 *The Financial Times*, 'Poland names new premier', 11-12 July 1992.
74 *The Financial Times*, 'Sejm strengthens Polish PM's hand', 4 August 1992.
75 Ibid.
76 *Le Monde*, 'La Hongrie, un "capitalism du goulasch"', 28 July 1992.
77 *The Guardian*, 'Hungarians abroad fear their hosts' long-term wrath', 13 June 1992.
78 *Le Monde*, 'Le governement prépare un projet de loi sur les droits des minorités', 16 June 1992.
79 Sam Cohen in *The Christian Science Monitor*, 'Turkey Still Positive Despite EC Rebuff', 4 January 1990.
80 *The Financial Times Survey*, 'Turkey', 21 May 1992.
81 *Europe*, 27 June 1992, No. 5759, p. 14.
82 Seyfi Tashan, *Turkey from Marginality to Centrality*, paper given at Anglo-Turkish Round Table, Chatham House, January 1992.
83 Mehmet Öğütcü, 'Turkey's Place in the New Architecture of Europe: An Updated Assessment', unpublished paper, College of Europe, Bruges, April 1992.
84 European Council in Lisbon, 26/27 June 1992, 'Conclusions of the Presidency', in *Europe*, Special Edition No. 5760, 28 June 1992.
85 *Europe*, 24 July 1992, No. 5778, p. 5.
86 *Europe*, 20/21 July 1992, No. 5776, p. 4.
87 *The Financial Times*, 'Germany halts arms to Turkey', 27 March 1992. See also *The Financial Times*, 3 April 1992, and *The Independent*, 1 April 1992.
88 *Europe*, 15 July 1992, No. 5772.
89 François Mitterrand, *Statements ... in the course of his joint press conference with President Turgut Ozal*, Istanbul, 14 April 1992.
90 *The Financial Times*, 'Hurd seeks to reassure Turkey', 22 April 1992.
91 *The Financial Times Survey*, 'Turkey', 21 May 1992.
92 *Europe*, 27 June 1992, No. 5759, p. 7.

93 On Maltese relations with the EC, see *The Financial Times Survey*, 28 January 1991, and 6 November 1990, 'Malta embraces a market culture'; also *Le Monde*, July 18 1990, 'Malte a deposé sa demande d'adhésion à la CE'.

94 *Le Monde*, 17 October 1989, 'Malte aux portes de la CE'.

95 *The Financial Times Survey*, 'Malta', op cit. (n. 93).

96 Eurostat/EFTA, op cit. (n. 2).

97 *The Financial Times*, 21 February 1992, 'EC is key issue in Malta poll'.

98 Constantine Stephanou and Charalambos Tsardanides, 'The EC and Greece–Turkey–Cyprus', in Constas (ed.), *The Greek–Turkish Conflict in the 1990s*, Macmillan, London, 1991.

99 European Parliament, *Resolution on the Situation in Cyprus*, doc. A2-317/87.

100 *Europe*, 18 July 1992, No. 5775, p. 4.

101 Quoted in *Cyprus Bulletin*, 'Cyprus applies for EC membership', 4 July 1990.

102 *The Financial Times Survey*, 'Republic of Cyprus', 23 March 1992.

103 *Le Monde*, 'Chypre, candidat impatient', 8 September 1992; *Europe*, 7 August 1992, No. 5788, p. 3.

104 *The Financial Times Survey*, op cit. (n. 102).

Chapter 4

1 For detailed accounts of the background of the EFTA-EC relationship, see Thomas Pedersen, *The Wider Western Europe: EC Policy Towards the EFTA Countries*, RIIA Discussion Paper No. 10, RIIA, London, 1988; and Wallace (ed.), *The Wider Western Europe*.

2 *The Financial Times*, 27 January, 4 February, 14 February and 2/3 May 1992, and *Europe* 16/17 December 1991, 3/4 February and 6 February 1992.

3 This discussion draws on: Helen Wallace and Wolfgang Wessels in Wallace (ed.), *The Wider Western Europe*; Helen Wallace, 'Vers un espace économique européen: chances et difficultés d'une négociation conclue au finish', *Revue du Marché Commun*, November 1991; and Helen Wallace, 'The European Economic Area: A common market in search for a political vision', in *Europe in Search of a map*, Project Promethée Perspectives, No. 2, Promethée, Paris, April 1992.

4 Ulf Dinkelspiel in House of Lords, Select Committee on the

European Communities, 14th Report *Relations between the Community and EFTA*, HL Paper 55-II, HMSO, London, 1990.

5   Avis de la Cour du 14 décembre 1991, Avis 1/91, *Projet d'accord entre la Communauté, d'une part, et les pays de l'Association Européenne de Libre Echange, d'autre part, portant sur la création de l'Espace Economique Européen.*

6   Agreement on the European Economic Area.

7   *Europe*, No. 5660, 3/4 February 1992, and No. 5662, 6 February 1992, and *The Financial Times*, 4 February 1992.

8   See, for instance, Josef Brada, 'The European Community and Czechoslovakia, Hungary, and Poland', *Report on Eastern Europe*, 6 December 1991; Heinz Kramer, 'The EC and Stabilisation of Eastern Europe', *Aussenpolitik*, Vol. 42, January 1992; and Richard Portes, 'The Impact of Eastern Europe on the European Community', paper presented at a CEPR conference, 20–21 March 1992.

9   On cooperation among central and east European countries, see Libor Roucek, *After the Bloc : The New International Relations in Eastern Europe*, RIIA Discussion Paper No. 40, RIIA, London, 1992.

Appendix One

Population and trade

Table 1: Population of EC member states (mid-year estimates in millions)

	1988	1989	1990	1991	2000
Belgium	9.9	9.9	9.9	9.9	9.8
Denmark	5.2	5.2	5.2	5.2	5.1
(West) Germany	60.8	60.8	60.8	60.8	59.2
Greece	10.1	10.2	10.2	10.2	10.4
Spain	39.9	40.2	40.4	40.5	40.7
France	55.9	55.6	55.4	55.6	57.9
Ireland	3.7	3.8	3.8	3.8	4.1
Italy	57.2	57.3	57.3	57.3	57.2
Luxembourg	0.4	0.4	0.4	0.4	0.4
Netherlands	14.6	14.7	14.8	14.9	15.2
Portugal	10.3	10.3	10.4	10.4	11.1
United Kingdom	55.7	55.7	55.9	56.0	57.7

Table 2: Population of possible future members of the EC (mid-year estimates in millions)

	1988	1989	1990	1991	2000
EC12*	340.78	342.10	343.72	344.90	351.30
Austria	7.60	7.62	7.71	7.80	7.70
Finland	4.95	4.96	4.99	5.00	5.10
Norway	4.21	4.23	4.24	4.30	4.30
Sweden	8.44	8.49	8.56	8.60	8.50
Switzerland	6.59	6.65	6.71	6.80	6.80
Total	31.79	31.95	32.21	32.50	32.40
Cyprus	0.69	0.69	0.70	0.70	0.80
Malta	0.35	0.35	0.35	0.35	0.40
Turkey	53.71	54.89	56.10	59.90	70.00
Total	54.75	55.93	57.15	60.95	71.20
Albania	3.14	3.20	3.25	—	4.00
Bulgaria	8.98	8.99	9.01	8.82	9.00
Czechoslovakia	15.61	15.64	15.67	15.75	16.00
Hungary	10.60	10.58	10.55	10.56	10.30
Poland	37.86	37.85	38.42	38.38	40.50
Romania	23.05	23.15	23.27	23.26	24.40
Yugoslavia	23.55	23.69	23.83	23.97	25.20
Total	122.79	123.10	124.00	—	129.40
Estonia	—	1.57	—	—	—
Latvia	—	2.68	—	—	—
Lithuania	—	3.69	—	—	—
Total	—	7.94	—	—	—

* Includes former GDR.
Sources: 1988 to 1990: *Monthly Bulletin of Statistics*, UN, December 1991 (all countries except EC12 and Yugoslavia) and *European Economy no. 50*, DG II (EC12); 1991 and Yugoslavia: *World Economic Outlook*, WEFA, Paris, January 1992; 2000: *PC Globe*.

Table 3: EFTA trade in billion US $

Partner	1989 Imports	1989 Exports	1989 Balance	1990 Imports	1990 Exports	1990 Balance
World	195717	187321	-8396	229926	225512	-4414
EC12	112691	100680	-12011	135230	124271	-10959
Indu excl EC12	51830	50441	-1389	59850	58300	-1550
CEEC-7	3470	3851	381	4003	4565	562
DC	16396	18020	1624	18024	22241	4217

Notes: Indu excl EC12: industrial countries, EC12 excluded; CEEC-7:
Albania, Bulgaria, Czechoslovakia, Hungary, Poland, Romania,
Yugoslavia; DC: developing countries.
Source: COMTRADE data base, UN.

Table 4: Med-3 trade in billion US $

Partner	1989 Imports	1989 Exports	1989 Balance	1990 Imports	1990 Exports	1990 Balance
World	18069	12124	-5945	24864	13532	-11332
EC12	7017	5518	-1499	10273	6983	-3290
Indu excl EC12	4812	1847	-2965	5814	2021	-3793
CEEC-7	164	497	333	242	522	280
DC	4136	3422	-714	5465	2998	-2467

Notes: MED-3: Cyprus, Malta, Turkey; Indu excl EC12: industrial
countries, EC12 excluded; CEEC-7: Albania, Bulgaria, Czechoslovakia,
Hungary, Poland, Romania, Yugoslavia; DC: developing countries
Source: COMTRADE data base, UN.

Table 5: CEEC-7 trade in billion US $

Partner	1989			1990		
	Imports	Exports	Balance	Imports	Exports	Balance
World	33898	36434	2536	35722	37606	1884
EC12	11685	11544	-141	14319	15809	1490
Indu excl EC12	5862	5799	-63	7047	6385	-662
EFTA	3851	3470	-381	4565	4003	-562
DC	3577	3614	37	3810	3536	-274

Notes: Indu excl EC12: industrial countries, EC12 excluded; CEEC-7:
Albania, Bulgaria, Czechoslovakia, Hungary, Poland, Romania,
Yugoslavia; DC: developing countries.
Source: COMTRADE data base, UN.

Appendix Two

European Council in Lisbon, 26–27 June 1992

Extract from the Conclusions of the Presidency.

2 Enlargement

A The Treaty on European Union provides that any European State
whose system of government is founded on the principle of democracy may apply to become a member of the Union. The principle of a
Union open to European States that aspire to full participation and
who fulfil the conditions for membership is a fundamental element of
the European construction.

    The European Council in Maastricht agreed that negotiations on
accession to the Union on the basis of the Treaty agreed in Maastricht
can start as soon as the Community has terminated its negotiations on
Own Resources and related issues in 1992.

B The European Council considers that the EEA-agreement has paved
the way for opening enlargement negotiations with a view to an early
conclusion with EFTA countries seeking membership of the European
Union. It invites the institutions to speed up preparatory work needed
to ensure rapid progress including the preparation before the European Council in Edinburgh of the Union's general negotiation framework. The official negotiation will be opened immediately after the
Treaty on European Union is ratified and the agreement has been
achieved on the DELORS-II package.

    Negotiations with the candidate countries will, to the extent pos-
sible, be conducted in parallel, while dealing with each candidature on
its own merit.

    The European Council agrees that this enlargement is possible on the basis of the institutional provisions contained in the Treaty on the Union and attached declarations.

C   The European Council considers that if the challenges of a European Union composed of a larger number of Member States are to be met successfully, parallel progress is needed as regards the internal development of the Union and in preparation for membership of other countries.

In this context the European Council discussed the applications which have been submitted by Turkey, Cyprus and Malta. The European Council agrees that each of these applications must be considered on its merits.

With regard to Turkey the European Council underlines that the Turkish role in the present European political situation is of the greatest importance and that there is every reason to intensify cooperation and develop relations with Turkey in line with the prospect laid down in the Association Agreement of 1964 including a political dialogue at the highest level. The European Council asks the Commission and the Council to work on this basis in the coming months.

Relations with Cyprus and Malta will be developed and strengthened by building on the association agreements and their application for membership and by developing the political dialogue.

As regards relations with Central and Eastern Europe, the European Council reaffirms the Community's will to develop its partnership with these countries within the framework of the Euro-agreements in their efforts to restructure their economies and institutions. The political dialogue will be intensified and extended to include meetings at the highest political level. Cooperation will be focused systematically on assisting their efforts to prepare the accession to the Union which they seek. The Commission will evaluate progress made in this respect and report to the European Council in Edinburgh suggesting further steps as appropriate.

The Commission presented its report 'Europe and the challenge of enlargement'. This report is added to the conclusions of the European Council.

Appendix Three

Europe and the Challenge of Enlargement

A report from the Commission of the European Communities to the European Council, Lisbon, 24 June 1992.

Introduction

1   The European Council in Maastricht on 9–10 December 1991 noted that:

> The Treaty on European Union, which the Heads of State and Government have now agreed, provides that any European State whose system of Government is founded on the principle of democracy may apply to become a member of the Union. Negotiations on accession to the European Union on the basis of the Treaty now agreed can start as soon as the Community has terminated its negotiations on Own Resources and related issues in 1992. A number of European countries have submitted applications or announced their intention of seeking membership of the Union. The European Council invites the Commission to examine those questions, including the implications for the Union's future development, with regard to the European Council in Lisbon.

2   This report responds to that request. It aims to summarise the questions and clarify the debate now engaged in the Community institutions. It is based on the assumption that, as the European Council stated, accession will be to the Union on the basis of the Maastricht Treaty.

3   The European Community, having grown from six to twelve members, again faces the challenge of enlargement. Seven countries have applied for membership (Turkey, Cyprus, Malta, Austria, Sweden,

Finland, Switzerland), and others have announced their intention to apply. The question is thus posed of a Community of twenty, thirty or more members, even without the new independent states of the former Soviet Union, which are not covered in this report.

The new context

4   The accession of new members will be to a Community with new characteristics:

   – the completion of the single market, without internal frontiers;
   – the creation of the European Union;
   – economic and monetary union, and the move to a single currency;
   – the introduction of a common foreign and security policy.

5   The external context has also changed dramatically. The division which resulted from the Cold War has come to an end, and the countries concerned have embarked on the path of democratic and economic reform. The integration of these new democracies into the European family presents a historic opportunity. In the past, enlargement of the Community took place in a divided continent; in future, it can contribute to the unification of the whole of Europe. The Community has never been a closed club, and cannot now refuse the historic challenge to assume its continental responsibilities and contribute to the development of a political and economic order for the whole of Europe.

Deepening and widening

6   The important developments which were decided at Maastricht have still to be consolidated. The new Treaty has to be ratified, and the negotiations on the second package of financial and structural measures have to be completed. The accession negotiations, which can then commence, must be conducted in such a way as to contribute to the strengthening of the Union. The accession of new members will increase its diversity and heterogeneity. But widening must not be at the expense of deepening. Enlargement must not be a dilution of the Community's achievements. On this point there should be absolute clarity, on the part of the member states and of the applicants.

Conditions for new members

The limits of Europe

7 Article 237 of the Rome Treaty, and Article O of the Maastricht Treaty, say that 'any European state may apply to become a member'. The term 'European' has not been officially defined. It combines geographical, historical and cultural elements which all contribute to the European identity. The shared experience of proximity, ideas, values, and historical interaction cannot be condensed into a simple formula, and is subject to review by each succeeding generation. The Commission believes that it is neither possible nor opportune to establish now the frontiers of the European Union, whose contours will be shaped over many years to come.

Conditions and criteria

8 Other essential characteristics of the Union, referred to in Article F of the Maastricht Treaty, are the principles of democracy and the respect of fundamental human rights. A state which applies for membership must therefore satisfy the three basic conditions of European identity, democratic status, and respect of human rights.

9 Another set of criteria relates to the applicant state's acceptance of the Community system, and its capacity to implement it. As the Community's legal, economic, and political framework has developed, the obligations of membership have become progressively more difficult to fulfil. The obligations presuppose a functioning and competitive market economy, and an adequate legal and administrative framework in the public and the private sector. An applicant country without these characteristics could not be effectively integrated; in fact, membership would be more likely to harm than to benefit the economy of such a country, and would disrupt the working of the Community.

10 Applicant states should also accept, and be able to implement, the Common Foreign and Security Policy as it evolves over the coming years. An applicant country whose constitutional status, or stance in international affairs, rendered it unable to pursue the project on which the other members are embarked could not be satisfactorily integrated into the Union. It will be necessary to avoid ambiguity or misunderstanding on this point in the context of enlargement.

The Community's 'acquis'

11 Membership implies the acceptance of the rights and the obligations, actual and potential, of the Community system and its institutional framework – the Community's *acquis*, as it is known. That means:

 – the contents, principles and political objectives of the Treaties, including the Maastricht Treaty;
 – the legislation adopted in implementation of the Treaties, and the jurisprudence of the Court;
 – the declarations and resolutions adopted in the Community framework;
 – the international agreements, and the agreements between member states connected with the Community's activities.

12 The assumption of these rights and obligations by a new member may be subject to such technical adaptations, temporary (not permanent) derogations, and transitional arrangements as are agreed in accession negotiations. The Community will show comprehension for the problems of adjustment which may be posed for new members, and will seek adequate solutions. But the principle must be retained of acceptance of the *acquis*, to safeguard the achievements of the Community.

13 Future accessions will take place in conditions different from the past:

 – The completion of the single market means that the maintenance of frontiers between old and new members, even for a temporary period, could create problems. Such transitional arrangements should be kept to a strict minimum.
 – The realisation of economic and monetary union will imply a real effort of cohesion and solidarity on the part of all members. The passage to the final stage will depend on the number of states – including new members – who fulfil the criteria of economic convergence.
 – The *acquis* in the field of foreign policy and security will include the Maastricht Treaty and its political objectives.

Common Policies

14 Each accession requires a detailed evaluation of implications for the policies of the Community and the Union, and for the applicant country. Such an exercise is not possible in the scope of this report: it can be conducted on the basis of the Opinions, which the Commission has to make on each application.

15 However, it is evident that, among the applicant countries and potential applicants, some are relatively well-placed to take on the obligations of membership, while others are manifestly not in a position to adopt them in the near future.

16 From the economic point of view, the EFTA countries already have a high degree of integration with the Community, and with the agreement on the European Economic Area will adopt a large part of the Community's *acquis*. Their integration into the Community system would not pose insurmountable problems, either for them or for the existing member states, although it should be noted that there remain a number of sensitive fields, including those not covered by the European Economic Area, in which there may be difficulties. Likewise, the integration of Cyprus and Malta into the Community system would not pose insurmountable problems of an economic nature.

17 The Maastricht Treaty provides in Articles J.1–10 for the definition and implementation of a common foreign and security policy, which 'shall include all questions related to the security of the Union, including the eventual framing of a common defence policy, which might in time lead to a common defence'. Members of the Union will subscribe, in principle and in practice, to these provisions and have to implement the decisions taken under the Treaties. Applicant countries should be left with no doubts in this respect. Specific and binding assurances will be sought from them with regard to their political commitment and legal capacity to fulfil the obligations.

Safeguarding the Community's effectiveness

18 The impact of future enlargement on the capacity of the Community to take decisions merits the most careful reflection and evaluation. Non-members apply to join because the Community is attractive; the Community is attractive because it is seen to be effective; to proceed to enlargement in a way which reduces its effectiveness would be an error.

19 In the perspective of enlargement, and particularly of a Union of 20 or 30 members, the question is essentially one of efficacity: how to ensure that, with an increased number of members, the new Union can function, taking account of the fact that its responsibilities will be larger than those of the Community, and that the system for two of its pillars is of an intergovernmental nature. In that perspective, how can we ensure that 'more' does not lead to 'less'?

20 The European Parliament has already commenced reflections on this subject, on the basis of the report of its Committee on Institutional Affairs. By the end of 1992, specific decisions must in any case be taken on the number of members of the Commission and of the Parliament, in the light, *inter alia*, of the size of the Parliament in an enlarged Community.

Subsidiarity and democracy

21 It is widely recognised that the Community institutions already suffer from overload of work and difficulties of decision-making, because of the failure to respect satisfactory priorities. This leads to the complaint that there is excessive interference by the Community in trivial matters, and an absence of leadership in questions of vital importance. Each new accession will magnify the risk of overload and paralysis, because of the increased number of participants and the greater diversity of issues. The prospect of enlargement reinforces the need for a more rigorous application by each of the institutions of the principle of subsidiarity, as defined in Article G of the Maastricht Treaty.

22 Such an approach would imply, in a Union with an enlarged membership:

- a less comprehensive and detailed legislative programme for Council and Parliament;
- a more balanced attribution of tasks to the appropriate bodies at the appropriate levels (regional, national, or Community levels);
- a clearer distinction between responsibility for decision and responsibility for implementation, which can often be decentralised.

Another precondition for the effective functioning of an enlarged Union, with more citizens, is a more solid democratic basis. Decisions taken at the Community level already escape, for a large part, from the scrutiny of national parliaments, but are not yet subject to sufficient democratic control by the European Parliament. The prospect of enlargement reinforces the need for reforms to reduce the 'democratic deficit', and strengthen the role of the European Parliament.

The Institutions

23 There are three essential questions which concern, *mutatis mutandis*, all the Community institutions, and all the pillars of the Union:

i) What methods of work? How to improve the preparation of decisions, which in an enlarged Community will involve more complex and diverse considerations?

The Commission will have to streamline its own organisation and methods of work in view of enlargement. The Council also must pay attention to its working practices, so as to ensure adequate preparation and conduct of meetings with an increased number of members.

ii) What number of members? How to ensure that, with enlargement, the number of actors is appropriate to the tasks and responsibilities of each institution?

For the Parliament, the relation between the number of seats and the population of member states needs to be rationalised, and the question will need to be addressed of the total number of seats. For the Commission, there is the question of the number of members; various options will need to be examined. For the Council, problems could arise for the functioning of the Presidency, if one takes into account its increased tasks in the Union.

iii) What arrangements for reaching decisions? When deliberations have to be followed by actions, how to ensure that such decisions are taken in an equitable manner, but without the risk of paralysis?

In the case of Council decisions to be adopted by unanimity, it is manifest that each new accession will increase the difficulty of reaching consensus. In the case of decisions by qualified majority, it will be necessary to decide in the context of each accession on the number of votes to be allocated to the new member state, and on the number of votes required for a qualified majority decision.

24 These examples are not exhaustive, and the situation of the other institutions and organs of the Community will need to be examined in the light of enlargement. For example, for the Court of Justice, there will need to be a reflection on the number of members, and on the attribution of work, so as to ensure the coherence of Community jurisprudence and avoid an overload of cases.

25 In the shorter term, for the accession of a limited number of new members, the institutional adaptations could be limited to those appropriate for decision under Article O of the Maastricht Treaty (accession procedure). With the prospect of a Union of 20 or 30 members, fundamental questions of decision-making and the institutional framework cannot be evaded.

Languages

26 Enlargement will bring additional languages to the Community, thus enriching its cultural diversity. But more languages will also complicate its work. In the Community of 12 members there are 9 official languages in normal use; in a Community of 20 members there could be as many as 15 languages; with 30 members there could be as many as 25 languages. For reasons of principle, legal acts and important documents should continue to be translated into the official languages of all member states. To ensure effective communication in meetings, pragmatic solutions will have to be found by each of the institutions.

Conclusions

27 For certain countries, negotiations for accession could be opened with the prospect of a satisfactory conclusion within a reasonable period of time. These are countries whose state of preparation for membership is well-advanced, and whose integration into the Community system should not pose major problems.

28 For other countries, a period of preparation would be necessary before the possibility of membership could realistically be envisaged. For these countries, the Community should use all available means, in particular its various forms of bilateral agreements, to promote their economic and social development in such a way as to facilitate their eventual integration into the Community. The deepening of the political dialogue with them should also be pursued.

The applicant countries

29 As the Commission indicated in its Opinion of 1989 on Turkey's application, that country would experience serious difficulties in taking on the obligations resulting from the Community's economic and social policies. In order to speed up its rate of development in the coming years, the association agreement should be more actively and effectively applied. The Commission recalls that already in 1990 it suggested to the Council measures to complete the customs union, to undertake wide-ranging sectoral cooperation, to resume financial cooperation, and to raise the level of political dialogue. Events have highlighted Turkey's geopolitical importance, and the role which it can play as an ally and as a pole of stability in its region; the Community should take all appropriate steps to anchor it firmly within the future architecture of Europe.

30 In the case of Cyprus, there is inevitably a link between the question of accession and the problem which results from the *de facto* separation of the island into two entities, between which there is no movement of goods, persons or services. The Community must continue to encourage all efforts to find a solution, in particular through support for the resolutions of the United Nations and the initiatives of its Secretary General. In the meantime, the association agreement should be exploited so that Cyprus is enabled to pursue its economic integration.

31 In the case of Malta and Cyprus, the adoption of the Community's *acquis* would appear to pose no insuperable problems. However, both are very small states, and the question of their participation in the Community institutions would have to be resolved in an appropriate manner in accession negotiations. The Commission will address this question in its Opinions on these countries' applications.

32 The accession of the EFTA countries who have applied for membership – Austria, Sweden, Finland, and Switzerland – should not pose insuperable problems of an economic nature, and indeed would strengthen the Community in a number of ways. The question of neutrality, and its compatibility with the common foreign and security policy, is however a particular concern.

33 The negotiations for accession of those applicant countries which can adopt the Community system without a period of preparation can begin as soon as member states have ratified the Maastricht Treaty and concluded the negotiations on own resources and related issues. The Commission considers that accession negotiations should be conducted separately, on their own merits, with each of the countries concerned. However, it will be necessary to avoid a series of accessions on different dates, with all the inconvenience that would cause for the work of the institutions and the conduct of Community affairs.

A new partnership

34 With the other countries of Europe who have not applied for membership, the Community is developing agreements of various kinds appropriate to their situation. That is the case for Poland, Hungary and Czechoslovakia, with whom 'Europe agreements' have been concluded; negotiations for new agreements are under way with Bulgaria and Rumania; agreements on trade and cooperation have been signed with the Baltic republics and Albania; and appropriate agreements should be envisaged in due course – when the situation has stabilised

- with the new republics which are emerging from Yugoslavia. For these countries, such agreements can offer the possibility of improving their economic and social conditions, developing their economic integration, and strengthening their political cooperation with the Community.

35 However, the countries which are not yet in a position to accept the obligations of membership have political needs which go beyond the possibilities of existing agreements. They desire the reassurance that they will be treated as equal partners in the dialogue concerning Europe's future. They wish to increase their security by strengthening their political links with Western Europe. The Commission believes that new means should be created for this purpose, building upon the existing 'architecture' of European organisations, so as to create a 'European political area'.

36 Various formulas have already been suggested, such as regular meetings between European countries at the level of Heads of State and Government, either in the framework of a confederation based on the Council of Europe, or through a conference of European states meeting at the invitation of the European Council. Another formula, similar to the 'associate status' recently created within the Western European Union, would be to associate other European countries as 'partner-members' in specific Community policies, with the possibility to participate (but not to vote) in certain Community meetings on subjects of trans-European interest.

37 For the countries of Central and Eastern Europe, the Community must engage now the process of economic preparation, even if their accession lies well into the future. The success of their development in the coming years will be of capital importance not only for their peoples, but for the stability of Europe. The chance to share more fully in the benefits of access to the European market, and the prospect of membership, can help to bring prosperity and peace to a region where unrest still threatens to erupt as a result of poverty, nationalism, and fear.

38 Therefore the 'Europe agreements', with their dynamic and evolutionary nature, should be exploited fully and even improved. Fields in which further progress could be achieved include:

- the development of the administrative and legislative infrastructure necessary for the functioning of the market economy;
- fixing of a calendar for the adoption of the Community's *acquis*;

- the strengthening of economic cooperation, including the transfer of technology, and better involvement of the private sector;
- participation in projects such as 'trans-European networks', support of private investment, etc.;
- an improvement of the trade concessions;
- measures in the field of free movement of workers.

The agreements provide for a political dialogue with the Community, which has already been launched jointly with Poland, Hungary and Czechoslovakia. They also provide for a review in the course of the fifth year. This rendezvous could be advanced, so that a joint stocktaking of progress can form the basis for the future strengthening and adaptation of the agreements.

39 The economic integration of the European countries requires the development of cooperation between themselves, as well as bilateral links with the Community. The Commission welcomes and supports the cooperation already undertaken by Poland, Hungary and Czechoslovakia, as a result of the Visegrad Declaration, and it hopes that a free trade area can soon be established. The Community should encourage all suitable forms of regional and interregional cooperation in Europe, with a view to the eventual creation of a pan-European free trade area.

The challenge of the wider Europe

40 Enlargement is a challenge which the Community cannot refuse. The other countries of Europe are looking to us for guarantees of stability, peace and prosperity, and for the opportunity to play their part with us in the integration of Europe. For the new democracies, Europe remains a powerful idea, signifying the fundamental values and aspirations which their peoples kept alive during long years of oppression. To consolidate their new-found liberty, and stabilise their development, is not only in their interest, but ours.

41 To this challenge we must respond with a strategy that is inspired not only by practical considerations of what is possible in the near future, but by a vision of the wider Europe which must be imagined and prepared in the longer term. That is why the Commission proposes a strategy of opening negotiations soon with those countries which are ready and able to join, and preparing the way actively for others who may come later.

167

Appendix Four

Possible presidency rotation in a much enlarged Council

België	Liechtenstein
Bulgaria	Lietuva
Československo	Luxembourg
Danmark	Magyarország
Deutschland	Malta
Eesti	Nederland
Ellas	Norge
España	Österreich
France	Polska
Helvetia	Portugal
Hrvatska	România
Ireland	Slovenija
Ísland	Suomi
Italia	Sverige
Kypros	Türkiye
Latvija	United Kingdom